words that water
flowers

katherine flynn plucinsky

HU
HOUSE
PUBLISHING

The stories and events that appear in this book are true.

For information about special discounts for bulk purchases contact:
abigail@heartsunleashed.com

Manufactured in the United States of America
Library of Congress Cataloging-in-Publication Data Plucinsky, Katherine.

Summary:
Words That Water Flowers offers readers a space to pause, breathe, and feel seen in their own journey. Like flowers surrendering to the seasons, we, too, can trust that each stage of growth is essential. Through introspective poetry and reflective prose, Katherine Plucinsky guides you through release, renewal, and return—back to yourself, God, and others. This book is a reminder that growth is both gentle and wild, healing is a process, and you—like all living things—are meant to bloom.

By attuning inward, you'll be guided through the process of uprooting what no longer serves you, clearing the soil to plant seeds of change and deep roots of self-discovery. Removing the weeds of fear and doubt will allow you to blossom into the life you truly deserve. With words that ignite courage, you are empowered to take ownership of your life and move forward with purpose.

From the darkness of the soil, you will rise toward the light that has been there all along. More than a book, *Words That Water Flowers* is an offering of grace—an invitation to trust the unfolding of the process and bloom into the person you are meant to be.

ISBN:
979-8-9928289-2-4 (paperback)
979-8-9928289-0-0 (hardcover)

[1. Memoir-Nonfiction. 2. Poetry. 3. Spiritual-Nonfiction.
4. Self-help-Nonfiction. 5. Transformation. 6. Empowerment.]

"This profound book explores the emotional landscape of transformation. Each piece is a reflection on the cycles of pain, hope, and rebirth, offering readers a space to pause, breathe, and feel seen in their own journey.

With lyrical depth and an unwavering tenderness, Words That Water Flowers *is a soul-stirring tribute to the quiet miracles of healing. It's a must-read for anyone seeking solace, inspiration, or a reminder that even the smallest seeds, when nurtured, can blossom into something beautiful."*

—Timothy Patrick, LPC
Mental Health Therapist

"'I believe in you.' Words that water flowers."

—Michael Faudet

To my Gardener
and the people who water my flowers.

Table of Contents

PART III

WATERING THE SEED / learning patience, presence, mindfulness, and balance

III. *WATER with MINDFULNESS*

IV. *WATER with BALANCE*

PART IV

REACHING UPWARD / *awakening to God as light and source of all growth*

PART V

GROWING TOGETHER / *cultivating a garden of connection and relationship*

Introduction

You'll notice a quiet wisdom in the way flowers grow. The orchid does not rush its blooming. The rose grows in unseen ways, slowly stretching its roots deep into the earth, trusting the process. The tulip knows that rain is as necessary as sunshine. The wildflower knows that it will be provided for. The lily surrenders to the seasons, trusting that each stage—the stillness, the breaking, the rooting, the rising—is all necessary.

Welcome to *Words That Water Flowers*, a collection of poetry and reflections that invites you into this same gentle unfolding. It is a journey of release, renewal, and return—back to yourself, back to love, back to God. Through these pages, you will journey through growth: clearing out the weeds, planting deep roots in self-love, nourishing your inner world with presence and patience, and watering yourself with mindfulness and balance. Sprouting out from the ground, you'll reach up toward the light that has been there all along and embrace the beauty of connection. This journey begins inward, deep in the soil of the soul, and unfolds outward, growing into something seen, shared, and lived.

As we grow and move through different seasons of life, we must give ourselves endless grace and compassion. No matter where you find yourself—whether you are letting go of the old, planting the new, waiting in stillness, or blooming in abundance—this book is an invitation to honor your process, to tend to your inner garden with love, and to always have the courage to begin again from all you've outgrown.

Each word is an offering, a reminder that growth is both gentle and wild, that healing is a process, and that you, like all living things, are meant to bloom. Unlike other self-help books that promise a quick fix and an overwhelming list of more things to do, this book is less about striving and more about embracing the natural process of becoming.

Words have the power to nourish or deplete, to help us grow or cause us to wilt. I've always been a lover of words. I've been captivated by their ability, given a specific order and selection out of thousands of options, to evoke an epiphany. To heal, inspire, and transform. The words we choose, especially the ones we speak to ourselves, shape the landscape of our minds and hearts, and therefore, our lives. You are the gardener, so plant wisely.

May the words on these pages ground you in sturdy soil, nurture you when life inevitably pours rain, and empower you to face any fear holding you back from the life you want to live. May these words unearth you when you need to be planted anew, revealing your resilience within to start again. I invite you to feel it all, welcoming the experience of the full range of human emotion. May you blossom into fearless expression, reaching toward the light with beauty and truth.

I desire to water, with love, the places in you that have been withered from pain. I hope these pages become a sanctuary—a garden where you find beauty and rest, and where each word feels like a homecoming and empowers your becoming. I hope this book is more than words on a page, but an experience. Give yourself permission to pause—to feel. Let what comes up rise to the surface. Mark the pages, write in the margins, let the thoughts linger. Our world doesn't often make room for stillness, but here, you are invited to slow down and truly listen. May these words water the garden of your soul.

WORDS THAT WATER FLOWERS

i believe in you

i love you

i'm sorry, that's so hard

i can't imagine what that's like for you

you're brave

i'm proud of you

i hear you

i see you

i see more for you

the world is better with you in it

you are allowed to feel what you feel

it's okay to take your time and rest

you are enough

you don't have to carry this alone

your story has the power to inspire others

there's beauty in your becoming

PART I:

REMOVING THE WEEDS

releasing what no longer serves

"When a flower doesn't bloom, you fix the environment in which it grows, not the flower."

—Alexander Den Heijer

You almost didn't notice.

At first, they crept in slowly, quietly. A few stray vines curling at the edges, a bit of overgrowth here and there—nothing to be concerned about. You barely noticed as the weeds thickened, spreading across the soil, weaving themselves into the landscape of your life. They became part of the background, something you stepped over, worked around, lived with.

You told yourself this is just how things are.

Until one day, you realize that you can't even see the flowers in the garden anymore.

The weeds have taken over. You step forward carefully, unsure of where to begin. The roots twist beneath your feet. Thick and wild, they've crept their way through the soil, stealing the sunlight, the nutrients, the water—everything meant for the flowers. Some vines have grown so thick, they've begun to look like part of the landscape. Some have taken root so deeply that they seem immovable, defying every attempt to pull them free. Others have lingered so long, they almost feel like they belong.

And now, you're beginning to see it.

Maybe for the first time, you notice how thick and tangled everything has become. The soil beneath your feet is dried out and hardened. You reach down, running your hands through it, feeling how depleted it is. This is no longer a place of beauty, color, and life. It is a place of survival.

But gardens are not meant to survive. They are meant to flourish.

Before anything new can grow, the soil must be cleared.

Just as weeds take over, false narratives, unresolved pain, and patterns you've always lived with can spread quietly through your life, suffocating what you're trying to cultivate. Clearing the soil isn't just about removing what no longer serves you. It's about making space for something better.

This chapter is about pulling the weeds in your life: the stories you've told yourself, the habits that keep you small, the relationships, jobs, or circumstances that no longer nourish you. Maybe you've clung to them because they're familiar and it's easier than having to unearth them. But real growth starts when you face these things head-on and take responsibility for shifting them, rather than choosing to remain in your misery and complain about things you have the power to change.

As you kneel in the dirt, hands deep in hardened soil, tugging at stubborn roots, know this: The work of clearing is messy. It's exposing. It's exhausting. And at times, it's lonely.

But with each weed removed, you create space.

Space for what is meant to bloom.

BETTER THINGS

"how do you know
better things
are coming?" he asked.

"because
i've experienced it.

once you get out of that stagnant place
you're so afraid of leaving,
there's an entire life
w a i t i n g for you.

it's the most terrifying thing
you'll ever do.
but once you do,
you'll be amazed at how long it took you.

& of all of the things
you fear you'll regret,
it will be
that you didn't do it
sooner."

THE SUNFLOWER

she couldn't stop it.
nature kept stretching her,
taller and taller.

she tried everything
to resist change—
wrapping her vines tightly around the fence,
digging her roots deeper into the ground,
slouching to not absorb water from the rain,
holding her breath from the sunshine.

the tulips around her gossiped,
"she's changed."

attempting to make herself as small as possible,
she questioned,
"we're supposed to,
right?"
why were none of the other flowers
growing alongside her?
what did she need to do
to remain with them?

eventually, she reached a point too high
to hear the other flowers
murmuring criticism
beneath her.

she felt completely alone
in silence & solitude,
on the road less traveled.

it wasn't until a bee landed on her petals
and laughter poured out of her belly
from being tickled in a way
she had never felt before
sipping pollen
from her core.
the bee buzzed away with gratitude.

she realized then
she had a purpose
so much *greater than herself.*
all along
her changes,
her growing,
her healing,
it was never about
h e r.

it was about changing
to best be in service
to the world around her.

it was about
growing
in order
to love
more wildly,
to offer her gifts
more fearlessly.

self-love drips like honey
onto the flowers beneath her
because
when we fill ourselves up,
we can't help but overflow onto others.

she stopped apologizing
and allowed herself
to bloom with confidence
as she got closer and closer to the sun
and became a life-giving source
for the bees.

she began to love
the uniqueness
of being a sunflower.
an experience
the roses and tulips
may never know,
just as she would not know
the details that make up their journey.

the laughter up there.
    the purpose within.
            the warmth close to her face.

all along
she was not meant
to live close
to the ground.

there was more
awaiting her in the sky.

HEALING

THE WHY

Don't confuse the goal of healing with becoming perfect. Rather, it's to love better.

If we approach our healing intending to arrive at a flawless, idealized version of ourselves, we will have missed the point completely. Perfection is a mirage, an illusion that keeps us endlessly chasing what doesn't exist.

Ego whispers, "Change your flaws so you'll be worthy of love. Get rid of your baggage so you don't need anyone, and you can be more productive."

But love speaks differently. "No, darling. Heal to break cycles that hurt you and those around you. Heal, so the burdens you carry are lighter for the next generation. Heal, so your children don't have to. Heal, so you can love and heal others."

THE HOW

The deepest way to heal is by learning to honor all parts of yourself. How often do we misunderstand healing as a process of separating ourselves into categories by keeping the *good* and throwing out the *bad*, like sorting pieces of a puzzle? But real healing is integration— recognizing that every piece of us, both the beautiful and the painful, is necessary for the full picture. We don't need to rid ourselves of our humanness, but rather embrace the fullness of it.

Healing isn't about fixing or discarding the messy and flawed parts of yourself. It's about noticing, accepting, and loving the messy and flawed parts of yourself. Invite them to coffee, listen to their stories, and honor their journey. They've been through a lot, and they need your compassion, not condemnation.

And here's the beautiful irony:

Once these parts are seen and heard, they will naturally shift, change, and soften. They'll no longer need to shout for your attention, and their grip on your heart and mind begins to ease.

Softening toward your wounds with acceptance and compassion brings more healing than dismissing and judging parts of yourself in pursuit of flawlessness.

THIS IS THE SOUND OF CHAINS BREAKING

Don't mistake the chains that have held you in place, like stubborn weeds, tangled in and around the roots of your life, as security. They may feel like comfort, but they quietly hold you back, impeding your growth and your calling.

We all have patterns, relationship dynamics, routines, and ways of being that have influenced us for as long as we can remember. We've often existed within these unspoken, invisible lines for so long that it can be hard to tell where they end and we begin. But these things do not define you. You have the freedom to let them go whenever you choose.

No one may have told you this, but at any moment, you can decide to release what no longer serves you. You can step beyond the roles you've been handed, the routines you've been taught, and the beliefs that limit you. At any moment, you can change. You can move toward the life you're meant to live. Like God leading the Israelites out of slavery in Egypt to the Promised Land, you are invited into a life of freedom, peace, and abundance. But you must be willing to take the first step to leave what is enslaving you.

Sometimes, we find ourselves in the in-between—a foggy, uncertain space on the path between where we've been and where we hope to go. While aimlessly wandering in the wilderness, it's easy to romanticize the past, wanting to turn back rather than face the discomfort of change. We cling to certainty, even if it keeps us small. Even if we weren't happy, somehow, the predictable can feel easier than facing the unknown. Yet, God doesn't call us backwards.

Don't confuse chaos for connection. Don't mistake what confines you as safety. Trust that anything that lies ahead is better than what you've left behind. Like the Israelites, your children won't have to wander through the wilderness because they will begin their lives in a land overflowing with milk & honey. All because of your life's work to get there.

—*this is the sound of chains breaking*

YOU ARE NOT STUCK

sometimes you are your own obstacle

Life changes when you realize this hard truth: *No one is coming to save you.*

I spent so much time in my sorrow, waiting for someone to rescue me and do the hard things for me, the way I often tried to do for other people.

I continued giving away my power to situations and people that made me miserable, physically and emotionally unwell. I continued complaining about the same situations I was actively choosing to remain in. I was choosing victimhood. I was benefiting from being a people-pleaser because I didn't have to take authority over the quality of my life. I could keep blaming God, my circumstances, or other people.

The truth is: I was my own obstacle.

If you are not willing to do the hard things—if you are not willing to make a move, take action, make a change—no one can do it for you. It's not that the people in your life don't love you enough, but it's that they literally can't. No matter how badly they want to.

No one can make you *desire* change. Until that desire is there and you're willing to do anything for it, you will stay stuck. You'll keep complaining and coming up with excuses, letting fear drive your life. You'll remain in slavery to victimhood forever.

When you do finally realize that you are responsible for making a change, and you take that small course of action that only you can for your desired life, then all of the support in the world floods in. You were never alone. Suddenly, the walls of self-pity cave in and flood with empowerment and encouragement from the people who have been rooting for you all along. All you needed was that act of owning your power and taking back your agency, no matter how small. And then God does the rest.

Jesus often asked, "Do you *want* to be healed?" before performing the miracle. He waits for our response and free will.

We have to want it. We have to choose it.

COMPLETION

completion:

leaving something when it has
served its purpose in your life
and you are energetically complete with it.

when there is nothing
more for you
in a given place.

when you come to a state
of no longer being
energetically charged
by a situation.

acknowledging the end has come
for something, and it is time
to let it go.

being attuned to the natural end of something
by recognizing that you are forcing, or spending
more energy, on trying to keep it together
than following the invitation of surrender.

COMING OUT OF SURVIVAL MODE

you miss the predictability, even if it wasn't good / this is both
exciting and terrifying // waiting for the other shoe to drop / learning
to trust the ground beneath your feet // you're not numb anymore /
it's strange to feel everything so deeply // you can't stop crying about
things from years ago / you can finally exhale // setting boundaries
is harder than you thought / you feel lighter // you caught yourself
singing in the grocery store today / is this what healing feels like? //
you need so much rest but you feel guilty for it / "no" // the smallest
tasks feel huge / the world feels bigger // hypervigilance / constantly
reminding yourself you're safe // your old ways of coping aren't
working like they used to / you're finding peace in healthier ones //
everything feels unfamiliar / you're becoming okay with not having
all the answers // you're learning to move at your own pace / this life
is truly yours // do you deserve to feel this good? / it's okay to dream
again // it really does get better / it really does get better / it really does
get better //

PART II:

PLANTING ROOTS
building a foundation in self-love

"Don't wait for someone to bring you flowers.
Plant your own garden and decorate your own soul."

—Luther Burbank

The soil is cleared.

With dozens of weeds pulled, tangled roots now lie in a trash bag beside you.

After wiping the sweat from your face, you let out a deep exhale. Kneeling, you feel the cool earth beneath your hands. The ground, once dry and hardened, now welcomes you with its softness. An open canvas, ready for new life. As your fingers dig into the soil, it crumbles gently, the earth no longer resisting, but embracing the chance for renewal. You carve out a small space, just enough to hold the seed. It's tiny in your palm, but within it is the promise of hope, the quiet potential of everything to come.

You place the seed into the earth, its size small but significant. In this simple act, there is a commitment. You cover the seed with soil, pressing it gently into the ground, tucking it in as if to say, "You are safe here. I will take care of you." Nothing visible will change just yet, but in the unseen depths, something has begun.

This is the beginning of something beautiful. The seed, nestled in the soil, mirrors the foundation of self-love. It's the quiet commitment to take responsibility for the quality of your life, to choose compassion and gentleness even when it feels unnatural or hard. Self-love is not a quick fix but a slow, steady process that begins with doing the hard things for yourself. It's about listening to your body, even when your mind is filled with fear. It's the act of tending to your heart, even when you feel unworthy. Just like that seed, it needs care, patience, and trust to take root.

Self-love referred here is not to be confused with the fluffy self-absorption that leaves you empty or the hyper-independence that denies the need for others. This is deeper. It is an important truth that taking care of yourself is vital if you want to be truly present for others. Of course, you discover yourself when you give yourself as a gift to those around you. But to give authentically, you have to stop neglecting, damaging, and not listening to yourself. It's not sustainable to build others up if you're constantly tearing yourself down. When you ignore your needs, you wither inside. You become disconnected from the very life force that enables you to give.

The roots planted here begin with *including* yourself in your love. Without taking responsibility for yourself, your connections will leave you feeling empty, drained, or dependent, rather than supported and uplifted. Everything becomes a means of seeking validation. But when you nurture this seed of self-love with kindness, compassion, and respect, everything that grows from it—friendships, love, creativity, purpose—will flourish in a life-giving way.

As you plant this tiny seed, you wonder if anything is changing at all, if you're making progress or simply standing still. And sometimes, despite your best efforts, the weight of the weeds that used to reside here still takes up space in your thoughts and clouds your path. It's hard to tell if you're growing or just lost when everything still feels barren.

But this is the season of trust—the sacred pause between what was and what will be. A space both uncomfortable and full of promise. The dark is not abandonment; it is fertile ground. The uncertainty you feel is part of the process, a necessary shift that's taking place beneath the surface. It may not look like progress yet, but the soil is softening and the ground beneath you is beginning to settle. If you don't learn to take care of yourself now, you will wither.

The seed is planted, and with it, self-love begins to take root.

CLAY

we are clay
in the potter's hands.
our ways
are not set in stone.
our patterns,
the things that feel deeply inherent,
the survival tactics
and defense mechanisms,
our habits and our path:

it's all moldable
for restoration
by the Artist.

God's tears fall
from the deep pain
of what you've endured—

wetting the dirt,
now able to mold you,
into something *new*.

SELF - CARE

it doesn't have to be "me first,"
but it does have to be
"me, *too.*"

it is not prioritizing yourself
only,
but it is prioritizing yourself
also.

it does not mean we discount
others,
but it does mean
we stop discounting
ourselves.

katherine flynn plucinsky

SALTWATER BAPTISM

i spend hours in front of the ocean
u n
f o l d
i n g.

every minute spent
in saltwater
is a rinse
of what has been held in
all of these years.
letting it all
w a s h away
with each pull of the tide.
soaking in the very element
that makes up tears.

every sunset
i run into the warm water,
as pink paint is splashed onto the canvas of the sky,
diving under the waves
sinking beneath the surface
and coming back up
—it is a baptism—

i take a deep breath
and sip in the salty air
that births a new life.

SEEN

what they don't tell you about the process of learning to give yourself
the same love you give to everyone else is how empty you will feel at
first. how uncomfortable it will be. how all of your distractions will
vanish and you'll be left alone with the stranger in the mirror. how
wrong and selfish it may appear, how unnatural at first, like your
instincts and your body were not designed for this kind of love. how
much you will grasp at anything in your reach to fill the empty places.
how it will feel like dying at first.

but it isn't dying at all—rather, it's the birth of claiming a seat at
the table you never reserved for yourself. it's the dark soil before
you sprout out from the ground. for the first time, you are allowing
yourself to receive the love you so freely give.

i crave to be known
so i wash off what remains of my makeup from the day.
i make a pot of tea,
change into my comfiest clothes,
light a candle & turn my phone off.

i crave to be seen—
so i sit in front of the mirror.

i come to see;
and i come to be seen.

i gaze deep
into soft hazel eyes:
two windows
into an old soul
but a childlike heart.

brown galaxies
expanding into green constellations.
meeting myself,
for what feels like,
the first time.

i scan her face,
thinking she is pretty
in a sunday morning,
second-glance,
natural kind of way.

i see her story,
what she has fought to be here,
so many experiences in her little time here.
her pain, her joy,
her innocence, her wild.

i see goodness,
wisdom,
and depth.
so much depth.

i see resiliency,
strength,
and gentleness.
so much gentleness.

i see bruised hands that have grasped for control
and a voice, raspy, from crying out to God.

her body language appears sad,
a look i can tell
she doesn't let many people witness.

tears well up in her eyes
coloring them more green,
and her lips quiver
the way they do when she's trying
to fight back from crying.
but the tears win
as they blink out of her eyes,
she fights the urge
to wipe them away
remembering the voice of a therapist
who would ask her,
"why do you always stop your tears
before they can even make it
out of your eyes?"

so instead
she clasped her hands in her lap
and let her tears cascade gently,
dancing their way
down her cheeks,
stopping at her mouth
and dripping in
over the curvature
of her slightly parted lips.

perhaps
she stopped the tears at the corner of her eyes
for either way
she felt bound to swallow
the truth she ached to speak.

SEEN: PT II

of all that you've been through,
in ways no one could ever fully know,
i see how brave you've been
how hard you try
& how much you worry about everyone.

i see how difficult it is
and how you shine through it all
on your hardest days.
how you keep your poise and character intact always.
i see how tired you are
of hoping in God,
of praying for things to get better,
of seeing the best in people,
and waiting for your turn.

but more than being seen for your resilience, how strong you are, and
how brave you've been—i know what you're craving to be seen for is
how your gentle heart can't take much more. how the boulders you
put on your back are cracking your spine. how your once-soft heart
has had to harden to it all, but still somehow remains gravely fragile.
few people know, unless they take your tender heart into their hands,
it is broken open, barely held together by an array of bandages, feeling
every slight thing so entirely.

what you're craving to be seen for is not for how strong you've been,
but for how tired you are, what you have endured, and how you long
to rest. you're aware of your resiliency. you have proven your capacity
to find stars in the darkest of nights. you don't need a reminder about
your ability to bounce back.

what aches to be seen is not your strength,
but rather your pain.

–i see it

COMING OF AGE

i'm courageously creating space
to take care of myself,
and even more,
to not feel guilty about it.

because a good mother
and wife
and friend
and daughter
and sister
learns to process
and feel
and articulate
her emotions,
allowing
the people around her
to do the same.

ALL PARTS DESERVE LOVE

You deserve love when you're tired.
You deserve love when you're anxious.
You deserve love when you feel heavy.
You deserve love when you need rest.
You deserve love when you're not being productive.
You deserve love when you're sick.
You deserve love when you feel shame.
You deserve love when you've made a mistake.
You deserve love when you are lonely.
You deserve love when you cry.
You deserve love when you're not "on."
You deserve as much love on the days you can't get out of bed
as on the days when you feel unstoppable.
Remember, nothing in nature blooms
all year long.

Whether you are
budding or burning,
barren or blossoming:
You deserve love.
You deserve love.
You deserve love.
(all parts of you)

THE WOMAN EMERGING

when you begin to heal
a stronger and clearer self emerges
unveiling herself day by day.

i've never known the part of myself
who has access to the ocean as a support system—
she's willing to feel more.

i've never known the part of myself
that no longer caters to the approval of others—
she's not willing to abandon herself any longer.

i've never known myself to fight for my needs—
she's someone i'm learning to trust.

i've never known these parts
because all of this is new,
but the woman emerging
is someone who i'm beginning
to look up to.
she's someone who can give me
what i've been looking for all these years.

the days you hoped for
of sitting in the sun
and things not feeling so bad—
those days come.
and they come soon.

you'll come undone
time and time again
and you'll come back together
more beautiful than you could ever imagine.

THE PRIVILEGE OF AGING

you are not the same woman you were three years ago—your hair
is longer and colored lighter from the sun, you don't carry the same
heaviness, and you know how to walk away from what is not meant
for you. you are not the same woman you were last year—the light
came back in your green eyes and your baseline is joy instead of fear.
you are not the same woman you were a month ago—you're rooted
in the present and you feel more in your body. you are not the same
woman you were a week ago—you have a new favorite artist and you
are better at speaking your truth. you are not the same woman you
were even yesterday—you don't take yourself so seriously, and the life
you're building is becoming more full each day. you are more sure of
yourself with every sunrise.

—getting older is a gift

REBELLION IN RESTING

people who feel a need to fight for
and earn their worth
through productivity
are going to be threatened
by you
comfortably resting
in yours.

—*rest in your worth anyway*

TAKE UP SPACE

Why do you define yourself by the space
you do *not* take up?

The gap between your thighs, the smaller size
of jeans you squeeze into.
Always crossing your legs,
folding your arms.
The habit of sucking in,
not speaking up, holding your breath.

You have learned to define yourself by
your lack;
By the absence of space, of what does not exist.

I once resented how my body leaned into womanhood,
how hips curved where bones once peeked.

I longed for straight and sleek hair
instead of my messy,
voluminous curls.
The unruly waves and spirals framing my face
that felt too unpolished,
too bold,
a reminder of what needed to be tamed.

My being was becoming the very thing I feared:
something that took up space with the need to assert myself.
No longer willing to slip quietly by, unseen,
breaking the unspoken rules that once kept me small.

But I am woman—full, unhidden, whole.
From the shape of my curves
to the wildness of my curls,
the embodied message became clear:

"you were always
meant
to take up space."

Settle into your skin.
Embody your being.
Step into your fullness.
Stop shrinking.

To exist without apology,
without the need to fold inward,
to let curve and soul
take up every inch they were made for.
This body is a home I am learning to cherish,
not for where it lacks,
but for all the beautiful life it holds.

CURLS

"i love when your hair's natural,"
he said,
glancing at the messy curls
kissed by the sun
falling in front of soft, hazel eyes.

"you look more like
yourself.

lighter.

like you're not carrying so much
of the world's weight
on your shoulders."

TRUST YOURSELF

If you are looking for the answers, sink within—

Put down the self-help books and turn off the podcasts. You don't need to seek advice from everyone you know. We're so used to making other people the experts in our lives, while ignoring the wisdom within. Why do we trust their opinions instead of the truth that our own bodies are trying to reveal to us?

If you want clarity or guidance, let the noise of the world fade into the background. Close your eyes and breathe deeply. Shut the door and sink into the quiet of your own being. Feel the stillness. What is the knowing in your soul saying?

If you get quiet enough, you'll *know*.

Your life doesn't require some elusive solution waiting to be uncovered by a guide. The answers you're looking for don't always lie in someone else's hands. No one else has lived your experiences or carried your dreams. How could they possibly know what your heart truly craves?

Trust your gut. Trust the wisdom within you, despite being conditioned not to. Let your intuition grow louder. Learn to recognize that voice—the still, small whisper from the deepest part of you that speaks not in words, but in knowing.

It may be hard to recognize at first, but the more you listen to your gut, the more you'll learn to trust yourself and realize you have everything you need to navigate what's in front of you. We were taught to look outside for the answers, but real wisdom is found within. Every decision, every choice becomes clear when you take the time to listen—to your body, to the quiet wisdom it holds.

Intuition often doesn't speak in words like "yes" or "no," but rather as sensations:

A contracting, or an opening.

A leaning toward, or away from.

Anxiety, or peace.

Do your best with the information you have, and always know you can change your mind. Nothing is permanent. It's better to admit you walked through the wrong door, than spend your life in the wrong room. Intuition is subtle, but she is yours and she was designed to guide you.

You have the answer.

BUILDING A FOUNDATION

your late twenties are a strange and fascinating time
because everyone seems to be in a different season of life.
there is no singular path,
there is no universal *right*.
there are just different people
experiencing so many different things,
each writing their own story.

it's easy to slip into comparison
looking to your left and your right,
wondering if you're too late
(or too early)
measuring where you should be
(versus where you are)
and questioning if everything really is unfolding
the way it's supposed to.

it's easy to feel behind
but remember you've been busy building roots, too.
maybe the roots you are planting
don't look like moving in with someone
but rather tidying up the home you've occupied your whole life.
you're falling in love, too,
with the person you've fallen asleep with
and woken up to every morning.

the work is no less valuable.
it's all equally important
because the foundation you are building now
is what will hold you up for the rest of your life.

the infrastructure you're constructing today
will be the ground on which your future family
will dance upon.
each brick of self-acceptance, compassion, gentleness,
every stone of healing and health,
is forming the bones of a warm and safe home
filled with laughter, love, and peace
that one day your people will step into.

you may feel like you aren't following the itinerary,
overwhelmed by all the unknowns
while other people appear to be surrounded by certainty.
but here's the thing:
you are where the magic happens—

while your friends are buying a house,
> *you're making yourself your home.*

while your peers are finding their person,
> *you're becoming your own.*

trust the magic of where you are
right now.
your story is unfolding exactly
as it's meant to.
(as is theirs)

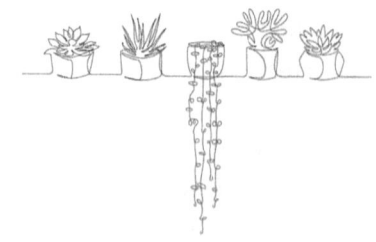

UNAPOLOGETIC

your boundaries are not negotiations.
your needs are not "up for debate."
your limitations are not suggestions.
you're allowed to assert what you require,
what you need, and what you want.

what you communicate is your truth
and it deserves to be treated as such.

it's not your job to make someone
agree, understand, or accept
what you will or will not do.

THE MOST IMPORTANT APOLOGY

I offer you nothing but grace, patience, compassion, admiration, gentleness, & forgiveness.

I forgive you for staying,
and I forgive you for leaving.

I forgive you for being harsh,
and I forgive you for letting people walk on you.

I forgive you for being paralyzed in your decisions,
and I forgive you for making impulsive choices.

I forgive you for being consumed with other people's suffering,
and I forgive you for feeling happiness even amidst other people's pain.

I forgive you for choosing someone else,
and I forgive you for choosing yourself.

I forgive you for doing whatever you had to do to survive.

I forgive you. I forgive you. I forgive you.
I forgive you. I forgive you. I forgive ~~you~~ myself.
For doing the best you could.

COMING HOME TO YOURSELF

At sixteen, you met a boy who taught you how to love yourself for the
first time.
At eighteen, you left for college across the country to discover who
you were without knowing a soul.
At twenty-one, life shattered and taught you about its frailty, and you
had to re-learn how to live.
At twenty-two, you dedicated your life to God and learned that it is
only through giving of yourself that you can truly find yourself.
At twenty-four, you had to learn not to give all of yourself away.
At twenty-five, you learned that family is everything.
At twenty-six, you followed your dreams and moved by the sea.
At twenty-seven, you put ink on your ribs declaring that you belong
deeply to yourself.
At twenty-nine, you opened the door for every past version of yourself.

On the morning of your 30th birthday, three decades of every woman
you have ever been pour in the door like sunlight spilling across the
room. They gather on the couch, placing your presents and flowers on
the kitchen table.

You welcome the dreamer, the worrier, the lover, the fighter, the one
who stood strong, and the one who nearly broke under the weight of
it all. They come with their scars, their wisdom, and their laughter.
They sip their coffee and tell their stories with knowing smiles and
open hearts. They celebrate you, the woman who stands here now,
because she sees that every experience, every chapter was written with
purpose.

At thirty, you breathe deeply, filling your lungs with belonging. All of
these women built the bridge that carried you here.

katherine flynn plucinsky

—at last, you are at home in your body

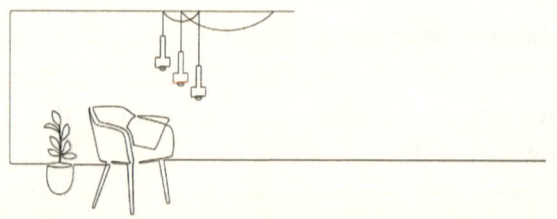

BE YOUR OWN ADVOCATE

Nobody is ever going to fight for your needs
like you are.

—*a reminder*

SANCTUARY

i have a place
to process,
to rest, to recharge,
to express, to feel.

this space is mine.
and there is only one rule:

you can keep your shoes on,
leave your dishes in the sink,
blankets are on the couch.

but do not enter
into my space
if you do not intend
to keep the peace
i worked so hard to create.

you don't have to bring your own food,
wine is always provided,
coffee is perpetually brewing.
come as you are—

but
do not disrupt
the safety
and warmth
that abides here.

SUFFER THE MISUNDERSTANDING

Stop explaining yourself.

When you realize you no longer have to justify or convince anyone of your choices or beliefs, this profound shift liberates you. You don't have to prove the validity of your feelings. Someone's disapproval is often a reflection of their own experience and perspective, not a credibility of yours.

Focus on honoring your truth, rather than persuading others to align with it. Trust your intuition, your beliefs, your instincts, and your experiences, honoring that you know what is best for you. Become so deeply rooted in trusting yourself that it no longer feels necessary to prove or explain to anyone who is set on misunderstanding you.

Remember, not everyone is going to understand or support your journey, and that's perfectly okay. One day, they might. Continue on your path, and let nothing disturb your inner peace.

—*suffer the misunderstanding*

SOLITUDE

I know I was made to be a lover, but there is something about being in my own company that is completely irreplaceable. The peace I find from sinking deep within myself is unmatched. I'll protect this time with my life. As I slip away, solitude and silence draw me closer, alluring me with an irresistible pull.

Solitude hands me a warm mug as if saying, "Stay a while." Silence wraps a blanket around my shoulders. We all exhale together in synchronicity. There's no need to be or do anything here. In this sacred space, I need only to feel my own energy, to listen to my own heartbeat. It is a place of nourishment so that when I return to the world of connection, I can give from a place of wholeness. It is in solitude that I truly meet myself, and in doing so, I can better meet my partner.

Yes, I am a lover by nature, a soul that finds beauty in deep connection and aches of the boundless love I have to give. But that does not mean I must give up my solitude. It can be both.

EMPATH

You were born with a heart that absorbs the world's emotions, like a sponge soaking in every drop of joy and pain around you. The space you hold for others is a safe haven where worries, hopes, and heartaches can settle. You sense every shift in energy, every subtle variation of emotion around you. In your gentle sponge way, you quietly clean up what others exude.

As you take on their shame, it turns into blame. What people say, how they feel, what they project; it instinctively sinks into your pores, soaking your core, consuming you whole. Filling the quiet places within you that were once your own, the needs and emotions of others entangle your roots, leaving you overthrown.

You find yourself shrinking, slowly losing track between your feelings and theirs, until the lines blur and you're left carrying a fullness that is not entirely yours.

But over time, you begin to notice the weight of it all—the way it has soaked in deeper than it should.

You learned you can choose what you do and do not let through. You stopped letting in the rain. While your empathy is a gift, it does not have to exist to your detriment. Your sensitivity and intuition to what's around you don't have to leave you drained and overwhelmed. When you learn to channel empathy properly, what you deem as your weakness can become your greatest strength.

You rinsed it all out, and you made pretty shiny *glass* to protect your open spaces, creating an oasis where your empathy can flourish without being depleted. The glass is not heavy or rigid. Light still pours through. No longer do you absorb the spills that leave you heavy.

The emotional energy of another bounces off of you, returning back to whom it belongs with greater clarity and love. You can hold space for others, without losing yourself in the emotional clutter. You can offer compassion without sacrificing your own essence.

& next time it pours,
you reflect—
not absorb.

you are not a sponge any longer, dear.
you are a resilient mirror.

THE TRUTHS NO ONE IS TELLING YOU
(in your twenties & beyond)

1. No one knows what they're doing. Some people are just better at pretending.
2. Feeling lost and lonely is just a part of the human experience.
3. The very trait you envy in someone else might be the thing they feel most insecure about.
4. You'll place your identity in many things.
5. They will all fail you at some point.
6. You learn who you are on a deeper level each time.
7. Faith does not equate to always feeling good.
8. You'll grieve your friend when she gets married and has kids because she'll never be fully yours again.
9. You'll then celebrate her evolution into a woman of superhero capacity for selflessness and love.
10. You'll learn to leave the places where you do not feel loved, after dozens of times of staying a little too long.
11. When you need a reset—open the windows, light a candle, play music, and deep clean. It works every time.
12. Trying your best does not mean putting an unbearable amount of strain on yourself. Your best is what you can do without harming your physical or emotional health, not disregarding them.
13. Keep believing in sudden positive shifts because things can change for you at any time. Trust that.
14. Don't go back to anything you had to pray your way out of.
15. You won't die from disappointing someone, even though it may feel like it at first. (It's just your ego dying.)
16. Comparison truly is the thief of joy. Your friend, who is a wife and mother, may fantasize about the freedom and spontaneity of your life, while you dream about having more structure and roots. Enjoy your unique season of life because seasons always change.

17. Buy yourself the flowers, the book, the flight, or the concert tickets.
18. Include God in every decision.
19. That rejection was a blessing in disguise. (Trust me, you'll be grateful the door closed itself.)
20. You'll be tempted to marry someone you're not happy with or stay at a job you hate just because you feel like it's too late to start over.
21. Please start over.
22. A thousand times start over.
23. The opportunities that may not look good on a resume will inevitably change your life.
24. You'll feel truly rich when you start focusing on feeding your intellectual, emotional, and spiritual life.
25. Dreams happen one step at a time. You'll end up writing the book, but start with something tangible like submitting a piece to your favorite magazine first. Momentum will build.
26. The best decision you'll ever make is the one that terrifies you. Follow your dream of finally moving by the ocean, even if you don't know a soul.
27. Luxury is small circles, a private life, and slow mornings.
28. At 30, it finally feels like things are just getting good.
29. Your life is just beginning!!

PART III:

WATERING THE SEED

embodying patience, presence, mindfulness, balance

"To plant a garden is to dream of tomorrow."

—Audrey Hepburn

With the seed now planted in the earth, beginning to take root, you rise to your feet and reach for the watering can.

The seed won't grow just because it's planted. It needs care.

This is where the real work happens, the daily tending to your inner landscape. Growth isn't born from a single breakthrough moment, but from the consistent choices we make each day of showing up. It's in the deep breaths, the way you speak to yourself every morning, the courage to continually let go of doubts that arise, and constantly coming back to meeting yourself with grace.

In the waiting, you do what you can. You learn what it means to keep showing up for the life you are cultivating, even when the growth can't be seen. It's not just planting the seed—it's sustaining it. It's the daily practices to care for your mind, body, and soul, even when it looks like nothing is changing. The daily task of watering reminds you that nourishment is both a gift and a responsibility.

The weight of the watering can feels grounding in your hands as you gently tilt it, watching the water sprinkle over the fresh soil.

Just as the seed needs water, you, too, need sustenance to grow. You slowly learn how to tend to your inner world by learning four consistent practices to hold you up:

Each day, you water yourself with. . .

Patience.

Presence.

Mindfulness.

Balance.

As the water sinks into the soil, these four vital nutrients sink into your heart and sustain you through the heat.

You rise from the garden bed, brushing the dirt from your hands, and set the empty watering can down. The seed remains beneath the soaking soil, hidden from sight, but something has already changed. You are learning to trust the process with greater confidence.

Slowly, over time, the seed will sprout. One tiny change at a time. But for now, you rest in knowing that you are doing the work, and the work is being done in you.

I.

WATER with PATIENCE

You return to the garden day after day, scanning the soil for any sign of life.

Each day, you pour *patience* over the place where you buried your hope. You continue to nourish it, even when you see nothing in return. You trust that something is shifting, even when the surface is still.

Growth is not instant. It happens slowly, in hidden places, long before it can be seen. The seed must break open before it can sprout—before it can push through the soil and reach for the light. And breaking open is a process that cannot be rushed.

Some days, it feels easy to focus on the journey of becoming rather than rushing to the destination. Other days, frustration grips you. But you show up anyway, choosing to believe that the unseen work will soon become visible.

You take time with each pour, embracing the quiet rhythm, trusting that the seed is receiving what it needs. The weeds sometimes reappear, but you remove them as they come, knowing that letting go, again and again, is part of the process.

Every day, you keep meeting yourself where you are with patience.

A MASTERPIECE IN THE MAKING

When I feel the urge to rush
my healing and growth—

I'm reminded that
You desire to take Your
time with me

For I am a beautiful piece.

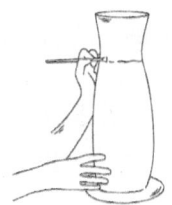

IN THE DARK SOIL

you don't eat the fruit
the day you plant the seed.

growth requires time—time to settle, time to root, time to unfold.
it's vital to give things time to grow in the dark, without rushing
or needing to understand the process. we don't need to witness the
process of growth to know that it's happening.

what grows in the dark
if not but babies and flowers,
seeds and ideas,
creativity and dreams?

what grows in the dark
if not but you and me?
our healing and relationships,
love and trust
all grow in places unseen
and unable to be measured.

a seed starts underground
surrounded by darkness,
protected from the world,
where it's nourished and given
the freedom to grow without interruption.
but dig it up to check its progress,
and its delicate unfolding will be disturbed.
open an oven too soon,
and dough will deflate and fail to rise.

a caterpillar grows in a dark cocoon
before emerging as a butterfly.
a baby forms in a safe womb
taking many months to become.

so, too, with our healing,
our spiritual growth,
our interior expansion,
the building of love with one another—
transformation happens beneath the surface,
in the dark and quiet within,
working its way through our being over time.

in honoring these quiet phases,
we release the need to control,
to measure,
to rush,
to understand.

when we make space for the natural unfolding
letting the darkness be the safe
untouched place
of gestation and mystery,
we can trust that all growth moves
at its own sacred pace and in its own time.

please, please
be patient
and gentle with yourself.

—*you're growing, even if you can't see it*

NEXT TIME YOU'RE ANXIOUS

on monday you had a panic attack.

you cried for two hours.
everything felt dark and hopeless, and you had no energy to do the
things that typically bring you joy.
you couldn't stop your heart from racing as fast as your thoughts.
the world was caving in on you.
it seemed like you would always feel this way and it would never end.

on thursday you watched the sunset as the sky turned shades of
orange and pink.

you swam in the ocean and let the warm salty air dry you.
you listened to a new album that just came out.
you felt full of hope.
you couldn't even remember feeling any other way.

—*it passes, i promise*

NEW YEARS RESOLUTION

It came to me on a drive...

My word for the year.

As it repeated itself in my mind, I was unenthused. It didn't sound as mighty or inspirational as some of my past declarations for the blank 365 days ahead.

My word: *fail.*

My great accomplishment this year will be... to fail.

It will be to fail over and over again because failing means trying, and trying means interacting with life. It means going for what I want with confidence, regardless of the outcome. Failing is the very thing that typically holds us back from making any resolution at all.

How often do we not even try to break a bad habit because we fear we can not do it? We assume within a month, we'll be back to doing the same things. How often do we hold back in relationships because we fear they will eventually end? Instead, we keep vulnerability and intimacy at arm's length. How often do we not create what we envision out of fear of it not being perfect? We shut down our dreams before even beginning, out of fear of criticism.

The fear of failing holds us back more than we realize. It doesn't just slow us down. It paralyzes us.

So I decided to go straight to the source.

I went to my usual coffee spot, and that's when I saw her.

Perfectionism.

Crisp blazer, leather notebook in hand, eyes scanning a spreadsheet that seemed far too detailed for a Saturday afternoon. Her posture was upright, spine like a ruler, hands clasped tightly in her lap when she wasn't making notes.

She glanced at me with a slight nod, and I realized—we'd met before. Many times, in fact. She was the one who kept me editing that email draft for an hour, who whispered "not good enough" when I tried something new.

I cleared my throat.
"Didn't expect to see you today."

She gave a tight smile. "I go everywhere you go. Someone has to keep things in order."

I wanted to hear her story and what had made her so afraid. Her voice trembled as she listed off what would happen if we didn't meet our quota for the year—the loss of love, worthiness, and esteem. She looked exhausted.

Before I could reply, a man with messy hair, paint-splattered pants, and mismatched socks flopped into the seat across from us. He was humming to himself, eyes twinkling, a sketchpad under his arm and a scuffed guitar resting on his back.

"Hello again," he grinned.

Failure.

Messy, unpredictable, loud.

He looked at Perfectionism and winked.
"Still trying to make life bulletproof, huh?"

She bristled. "Someone has to."

Failure chuckled. "The only way people learn is by falling short. It's in the cracks where the light comes through, and in the mistakes where wisdom hides."

Perfectionism's shoulders softened, and her breath deepened. Her demeanor changed as she let the idea settle: What if Failure wasn't her enemy, but her teacher?

This year, I want to become more comfortable with making mistakes and not doing everything perfectly. I want to open myself up to failure because I want to open myself up to life. This year, I will allow myself to make mistakes and not always have the solution. I will allow myself to try, even if it means I might disappoint myself or others. *God forbid, I will allow myself to be human.*

By the time we finished our coffees, Perfectionism took her hair down and slid her heels off under the table. She exhaled, and, for the first time in years, she let out a laugh. By the end of the year, I hope Failure rubs off on her a little bit.

FALLING & RETURNING

I believe the act of falling and returning is one of the most profound spiritual practices we engage in.

Life isn't a performance. It's a beautiful, messy, ongoing practice. It's about continually falling out of step, and choosing to get back in there. It's about the gentle art of losing and finding yourself in the ebb and flow of existence.

You're in a yoga class, shaking in a pose until you lose your balance and stumble. Each time you fall out of a pose, you have the opportunity to return—without judgment or criticism. You don't dwell on it or try to understand why you lost your balance, you simply let go of the fact you fell and return to the pose without it needing to mean anything.

The same thing happens in prayer or meditation. Your thoughts wander. Your focus drifts. And then comes the invitation to return, not with judgment but with grace. No need to label yourself as distracted or overanalyze why you lost focus. Just come back, as if you never left.

Through this lens, everything can become a spiritual practice. Life is full of these moments. Maybe you catch yourself missing someone who is no longer in your life. When you momentarily lose your grounding and thoughts of that person arise, it doesn't mean you're off track. You simply feel the ache, send love, and let go.

We get caught in various thought loops throughout the day. Each time you notice yourself spiraling, you can choose to let go and return to the present moment. You're practicing resilience. Playfulness. Grace.

You're learning to quiet the inner critic and replace it with a smile or a deep breath.

You don't stop working out because you missed one day. You don't stop pursuing a good habit because you failed once. Life is a cycle of falling and returning, falling and returning. And it's in the return that the power lies.

This year, may you embrace the tumble as much as the rise. May you learn to find joy in the fall, to meet yourself where you are, and to trust that every return brings you closer to your truest self.

GRACE

you redecorated your room—
painting the walls bright
and throwing out anything that felt like
a past version of yourself.

you sold your childhood dresser,
replaced it with a white oak,
and moved it
to the other side of the room.

some mornings
you still walk
to the left side of your bed,
reaching for a dresser that isn't there.

there is a simple lesson here:
grace.

if you still go left after two years of habit,
how much more grace, then,
do you need to give yourself
for the 5, 10, 20 years
of conditioning
you're trying to unlearn?

one morning,
without even noticing,
you'll go to the left
for the last time.

—give yourself an excessive amount of grace

II.

WATER with PRESENCE

Watering can in hand, you pour *presence* onto the seed as every drop soaks into the soil.

You slow down, allowing the moment to settle within you. You begin to notice things you hadn't before—the warmth of the sun on your skin, the way the breeze moves through the trees above you, the quiet hum of life all around you.

You grab a chair and settle into the moment outside, finding joy and grounding in simply being here. In this breath, in this space. Not in the future or the past. There's a lightness in this moment, an invitation to play. A ladybug lands on you, and it roams between your fingers. It's easy to become so focused on what's next that you forget to see what's already here.

You close your eyes, hearing the soft stream of water nearby, feeling joy rise within you like the first sign of spring. This moment is enough. Growth is coming, but life is here, now. If you spend all your time waiting for the flower to bloom, you'll miss the beauty already surrounding you.

You exhale, heart full, and hands damp with water and wonder. You feel grateful for the quiet unfolding of this present moment. For the gift of simply being.

Although nothing has broken through the soil yet, you realize growth is already happening—not just in the seed, but in you. You are learning to be present, to find joy in the process, and to trust that life is moving even when you cannot yet see the results. And for now, that is enough.

HOW LIFE FEELS > LOOKS

Focus more on how your life feels, rather than how it looks.

Move through life with intention.

Prioritize your interior state—your energy, your soul, your spiritual journey, your mental well-being, your intellect, and the quality of your thoughts—over how you appear to others, what you wear, how successful you seem, or how your life looks on social media.

Ask yourself:
What are you absorbing?
What are you creating?
What are you learning?
How are your relationships with yourself, others, and God?
What feels good?
What thoughts are you repeating all day?

Move your body because it clears your mind, not because you're trying to look a certain way. Run because it makes you feel strong. Exercise to connect with your body's power, not because it's something you "have" to do. Choose foods that nourish and energize you.

What would you do with your weekends if you didn't post anything about it? What would you choose to do if no one knew? If you focused more on how you feel and less on how you appear, would you invest more in experiences, like retreats or personal growth, than in clothes or products?

In the mornings, turn your phone on "do not disturb" and connect with a Higher Power before anyone else. Set an intention for the day, and don't tell anyone about it.

What if your decisions were guided solely by what feels right for you? What places, people, or habits would you let go of? Where would you start saying no more often, when your heart isn't aligned with saying yes? And in return, what would you finally say yes to that you've been putting off?

It doesn't matter how "happy" or "successful" you appear on the outside if your inner life isn't being nourished. When you focus on what makes your life meaningful and aligned, you begin to build a life that isn't just beautiful on the surface—it's deeply fulfilling at its core. You create a life that excites you, and become a person you're proud to be.

CREATIVE RECOVERY

You cannot create and criticize at the same time.

Because of this, as a creative of any kind, it's so important to nurture a relationship with your inner artist—the part of you that thrives on curiosity and self-expression. As children, we are naturally connected to this part of ourselves. We paint, sing, draw, dance, or build without hesitation; intuitively creating for the pure desire to express and explore. There's no fear of failure or rejection, no overthinking or analyzing. We color outside the lines and then come home beaming to hang up our work on the fridge. We eagerly share our creations with people we love, not to seek approval, but because these gifts are offerings from the deepest parts of us. Our confidence is rooted simply in the joy of creating and sharing.

After I published my first book, I felt a shift in writing. I started to become very perfectionistic with my work. Even my journals had to be well thought out. What had once been an act of joyful expression to make sense of myself and the world around me began to feel stiff with self-imposed expectations.

*Note: Journals are not meant to be polished places. They are the sacred space to vent and rid any and all chaos going on in the narrative of your mind. They should be the home of scribbles and crossed-oiut out words, and realizations and the only "aha's!" that can come from not knowing what's going to pour out onto the page in front of you from the week-long funk you've been in. Journals should be filled with coffee stains and dried tears from silly frustrations and deep anger, and so much rawness that you would be judged for speaking with such honesty in any other place.

This is why it's vital to reconnect with our inner artist, to nurture the childlike wonder, and create simply because it feels good to do so. I've grown to love spending time with this part of myself. I've found my inner artist to be refreshingly honest, a little rebellious, and funny as hell. (She ignores my criticism, I like that most about her.) I love her perspective on life.

She requires fun; otherwise, what's the point of creating if you're not enjoying it? She doesn't fixate on the final product or whether something is perfect. What she cares about most is the process: the joy, the curiosity, and the freedom to explore, learn, seek, and create. She needs room for what I used to call error, but now see as necessary exploration and growth.

So, I suppose this is what creative recovery looks like. Letting go of any perfectionism and criticism while you create, and learning to enjoy and trust the process. Creating and sharing, simply for the joy of it.

This is your reminder that while you create, through whatever outlet you enjoy, it does not need to be perfect, or even good by the world's standards. The most important thing is that it's authentic and feels good to you. People will naturally resonate with what's real.

Spend some time with your inner artist. Take them on a date and do something you've been putting off. Express yourself, without worrying about the outcome. Lean into this playful, fearless part of yourself. You'll learn a lot and you'll have way more fun along the way.

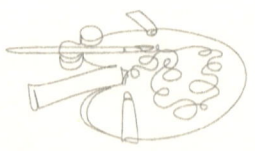

THE [BIG] LITTLE THINGS

I've devoted myself to a year of daily joys instead of holding out for the few big moments in a year.

A year dedicated to a daily hot yoga practice has shifted my physical and mental state. A year of daily beach walks, conversing with God, has elevated my spiritual life. A year of daily sunsets and documentation of the things that make me happy has made me more present. I spent 40 days collecting seashells and 365 days unfolding by the ocean. Sitting in the sun every day for 20 minutes & journaling gratitude before bed for 10 minutes.

These are the things that made my year. It is the consistent habits that build a beautiful life. Not the vacation, the weekends, or the dream goals—but the daily joys.

If you know that something inspires you, brings you peace, or makes you a more joyful version of yourself, why would you not go toward that? Why wait to save something for vacations, weekends, or daydreams—just 30% of your life—when you can make it a part of your everyday experience? If you know that you have limited time and any day could be your last, why would you wait?

"One day" might be "too late."

—fall in love with your everyday

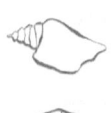

DON'T STARE AT YOUR WOUNDS FOREVER

You don't always have to dwell in places of pain to find healing.

Therapy, journaling, and reading about trauma have healed me in a thousand ways, but there comes a point when digging up old wounds no longer serves you. Your focus doesn't need to be constantly on fixing what hurt you. You'll be surprised at what happens when you stop digging. Healing comes when you start living again.

It happens naturally when you allow yourself to move on, instead of staying stuck in the past. When you let go of what's keeping you in pain, you can begin to embrace the goodness around you with both hands. Healing comes when you shift your focus from what has broken you to what is building you. It's found in the quiet decision to seek light, rather than dwelling in the shadows. In seeing beauty where pain once blinded you.

Healing often shows up in unexpected places: new people, new cities, and new experiences. You can let go—even if you never get the apology you deserve or fully understand why that horrible thing happened. Sometimes, the love and kindness of those who don't know your past will heal you just by their reckless, unguarded affection.

My deepest moments of healing have come from laughing until my sides ached and dancing in the living room at midnight with my best friends. It's not always in the big epiphanies or crying until your eyes run dry. Sometimes, healing is in the little things: drinking more water, taking a walk, getting into bed early.

It's in making yourself vulnerable again, even when it scares you. It happens when you plant your own garden, nurturing something new to life. You'll find more peace in spontaneous road trips or quiet mornings than in hours spent overthinking your past, trying to make sense of your suffering.

Don't stare at your wounds forever. The joy around you is waiting. Let yourself laugh, dance, and love again.

You've been hurting long enough.

GIVE YOURSELF PERMISSION

what if you give yourself permission
to start living before you have it all figured out?
would you embrace a heart broken-open
and hands still-bleeding
instead of staying on the sidelines
until you feel ready?
what if it's okay to start living
right now?

because what if we are never
ready,
or fully "healed,"
at least in the way we imagine?
what if we get to the end of our journey
realizing we wasted so much time
waiting for something in the distance to arrive?
not feeling ready or good enough,
staying inside,
when all along the point was to dance with life—
with messy hair, hands open, and a heart bleeding?

what if our broken hearts
are actually the point
of it all?

may you find joy
before you find solutions.
may you embrace laughter
even amidst your tears.
may you allow the messiness to be
part of your journey.

THINGS THAT MAKE MY HEART GO "!!!"

flowers / sunsets / slow mornings / rehashing a night out with your
friends over brunch / curling up on the couch with blankets on a
cold day / candles / going dancing / coffee dates / bubble baths / the
sound of rain hitting your window when you're falling asleep / "do
not disturb" / being with people that make you forget about your
phone / live music / deep conversation with strangers / cooking
together and sharing a meal with people you love / photography / the
quiet of the first snowfall / dinner parties / dog snuggles / fresh sheets
after a hot shower / people you can sit in comfortable silence with /
rooftops / finding an album you love front to back / sharing a bottle
of wine with someone you love / flow state / chips and salsa / the
smell of cookies in the oven / people who feel like home / the ocean /
you

STAY IN THE BEING

doing	‖	**being**
forcing, grasping, controlling		allowing any outcome to unfold while trusting that it's the best thing
chasing		being open to what's meant for you and allowing others the freedom to walk away
comparing		finding peace in following your unique path
explaining or proving yourself		accepting that others may misunderstand you
people-pleasing		trusting that you know what's best for yourself

—*stay in the being*

GRATITUDE IS JUST PAYING ATTENTION

If you want to cultivate gratitude, pay attention to what's around you.

The key to genuine gratitude is immersing yourself in the present moment unfolding before you. When you embrace present moment awareness, you shift from living on autopilot and going through the motions, to fully experiencing and appreciating everything around you.

Next time you visit home, notice how the feeling of your mom's hugs can fix anything in the world. Savor the smell of your dad making breakfast. Appreciate how lucky you are to be laughing with your siblings. Feel the comfort that comes from hearing your best friend's voice on the phone, even from a thousand miles away.

Take in the scent of the jasmine bush by your house that you pass every day, the one that smells amazing no matter how bad your day is. Appreciate the way your bones support you, and how your legs allow you to climb mountains, dance, and run. Tune into the feeling of youth in your body—how it holds you in this very moment.

For the love of the God who gave you these gifts, *pay attention*. These are the things you'll long for when tomorrow takes them.

Don't forget to capture the moment every once in a while.

SLOW

Slowing down is the easiest way to regulate your nervous system and undo trauma—

Sip your coffee.

Lengthen your exhales.

Open your hands.

Wait before responding.

Drop your shoulders.

Observe the pace of nature.

Walk instead of run.

Nap in the afternoon instead of drinking more coffee.

Soften your face.

Unclench your jaw.

Listen to the ocean.

Choose a yoga flow instead of a vigorous workout.

Let the salty waves float you.

Go outside and read poetry.

Sit in the sun.

Be present.

Feel your bare feet on the ground when you walk.

Take your time.

Sit with your mornings.

Put your phone down.

Meditate on your favorite line of a book before turning the page.

Celebrate each victory before moving to the next goal.

Let every sip of wine linger on your tongue.

Taste your food.

Close your eyes when you feel.

The sky is not falling. Nothing is as urgent as you think. Other people's demands or reactions are not as pressing and imperative as you have believed them to be. Nothing requires your immediate attention as if it were a matter of life or death.

The work will get done. People's emotions will pass. The world is not on fire.

—you have time

T(HERE)

be where your feet are.

trust that you are
exactly
where you need to be
in this very moment.

what's meant for you
will be there
when you arrive.

DESIGN YOUR LIFE

i love getting older

it's sunday morning and light is pouring in through the blinds, painting the living room a warm tone of calm. you're reading a book on the couch, the steam from your latte is rising to the tempo of jazz playing on the speaker. a beautiful boy is taking freshly warmed croissants out of the oven, filling the room with its buttery scent.

it's a monday and you're working in your pajamas on the couch with the christmas lights on. you have an endless supply of snacks and coffee right in the kitchen. you do a yoga class during lunch and walk to the beach for sunset.

these were the small moments i once dreamed of.

the best part of getting older is that you are finally in charge of your life. you can leave the places you don't want to be. no one can tell you what is right or wrong for you anymore. you can say yes and, thank god, you can say no. you can sign up for a random class. you can make the big purchase without asking anyone else. you can move your entire living room around to match your mood on a random tuesday, just because. you can lock the door and close the blinds and sink down into your peace. the wrong people and places don't get access to you anymore.

SOUNDTRACK TO THIS SEASON OF LIFE

The soundtrack to my current season of life sounds like waves crashing from my window and my neighbor playing guitar. It tastes like morning coffee, sipped slowly in pajama pants while watching the surfers dance on the horizon in silhouettes from the morning light.

This season of life feels like sand beneath my too often bare feet, grounding me to the earth as I walk along the shore, the first sensation of the day. My body, wrapped in a swimsuit, slipping slowly into the cool, crisp Pacific, only to be embraced by the sun's warmth afterward. Its rays are a soft, comforting kiss on my skin, reminding me that I'm alive. Here and now. The air carries the scent of salt and minerals, a fragrance of life beneath the surface. This season of life tastes like fresh fruit picked from the tree in our yard.

Living by the sea does something to you. It breathes inspiration throughout your day. You find yourself taking more pictures, creating more art, being more present, and going outside more often. No one misses a sunset. The pace of life is much slower.

Every moment is a symphony of sights, sounds, tastes, and textures that connect me deeply to the present, anchoring me in the now. It's a sensory existence that fills me with gratitude, a way of living I wouldn't trade for anything.

Mountains or ocean.
City or suburbs.
It does not matter, as long as you go where you feel the most alive—
go where inspiration dances in your bones,
go where you're excited to wake up every day.

Life is too short.

III.

WATER with MINDFULNESS

As time has passed, your mind begins to race: *Why has the seed still not sprouted? Can I really trust this process?* But instead of being swept away by the swirl of emotions, you take a deep breath and return to the earth beneath you. The solid ground steadies you. The metal of the watering can in your hands reminds you to be here, now.

With each pour, you water with *mindfulness*. You cultivate a daily practice of noticing your thoughts without clinging to them. They come and go like the breeze. Passing, shifting, never defining you. You are not your doubts. You are not your fears. You are the one tending the garden, steady and present, watching the seasons change.

You take a sip of lemonade and watch the water seep into the soil. You remind yourself that you don't have to believe everything your mind tells you. Instead, you learn to observe. To let the thoughts rise and fall, just as nature does, without resistance.

Some days, the skies darken. The rain is heavy and the winds harsh. You fear that what you've planted will be uprooted before it even has a chance to grow. But even the downpours, the unexpected chaos of nature, becomes part of the process. The soil is being softened. The roots, though unseen, are stretching deeper, anchoring themselves into the earth. The storm does not mean the seed is lost. It means the seed is learning to endure.

And so are you.

BREATHWORK

Breath sustains us in every moment.

Our breath has the profound power to soften hard movements and postures—physically and mentally. It slows everything down, quieting the mind and releasing tension from the body.

While learning to surf during a California July sunset, I paddled to catch a wave. But as I tried to get to my feet, I shifted too far forward, and the board slipped out from under me, throwing me headfirst into the water. I was caught in the break and held under by the force of the ocean's superiority. Panic began to set in as I reached for the distant surface, desperate for air, feeling far from it. I couldn't tell which way was up or down.

Suddenly, I remembered the voice of my yoga teacher from that same morning, guiding us through box breathing:

"ten seconds inhale—
      ten seconds HOLD.
ten seconds exhale—
      ten seconds HOLD."

Still underwater, I thought about the ease with which I held my breath only a few hours before.

Suddenly, my body surrendered to the water's pull, and a deep peace washed over me with the comforting truth, "You'll surface soon." My body softened, and my mind cleared. I heard my teacher's voice again, "Feel what it's like to be empty of breath—and let it be okay."

As soon as I let it be okay, almost effortlessly, I rose to the surface.

Isn't the same true for the waves of our thoughts, emotions, and the turmoil around us?

As soon as you can relax, it will pass and you will rise.

—*you'll always surface*

LET GO TO STAY CENTERED

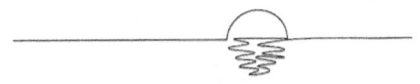

Your soul's most natural state is peace.

A deep, inherent calm lies within us all. This peace isn't something we can find outside of ourselves or earn through effort. It's always present, quietly waiting for us to return to it.

Every time we experience disturbance, whether it's a fleeting thought, an intense emotion, or an external event, it's as if a rock is thrown into the lake of our soul. The once smooth, glass-like surface becomes unsettled, sending ripples outward.

But these ripples are temporary.

The way back to peace isn't through reacting. When we try to manage, fix, or resist the disturbance, it's like putting our hand in the water and stirring it even more. We create additional ripples (thought spirals, frustrations, or anxieties) that pull us further from our natural state of peace. The harder we try to control the ripples, the more turbulent the water becomes.

Instead of intervening, I invite you to just observe. Become curious. Watch the disturbance without judgment, and let it pass through. Just like a rock sinking to the bottom of the lake, the disturbance will naturally settle if you don't engage with it. The water will return to its natural clarity, and so will you.

Letting go is not about ignoring or avoiding reality, but about releasing the need to control or resist what has already happened. It's a gentle relaxing, not from the mind but from the heart. By allowing yourself to remain centered, you stay grounded in your baseline peace. The ripples may move across the surface, but they won't touch the depths of your being.

And in this stillness, you'll find that peace was never lost. It's always waiting beneath the surface, ready to embrace you once again.

MEDITATION

If you step back for a moment and simply watch your emotions and thoughts as they rise and fall, you'll discover a profound truth—

You are not your thoughts or emotions.

You are the awareness, witnessing your thoughts and emotions as they pass. You are the still, gentle presence observing them all, coming and going like clouds drifting across the sky.

One thought does not have any more weight than another. Yet sometimes, a thought or feeling will provoke a reaction in you. You encounter something that doesn't feel neutral, something you either like or dislike. Then you cling to it, getting caught up in the narrative, and become entangled with it.

One moment, you are simply noticing a feeling of frustration, and the next, you're deep within its grasp. You let frustration envelop you, replaying old conversations, thinking about what you wish you had said. You become lost in your mind.

Meditation is a way to come back, again and again, to that quiet place of witnessing. Throughout your day, whenever you realize you're lost in thought, you can gently bring yourself back to the present. Instead of following every thought and emotion that stirs within you, let yourself remain as the observer, sitting calmly in the seat of awareness.

Imagine yourself sitting in the quiet, expansive space inside yourself. If you go deep enough within, there is a place behind all your thoughts where you simply witness everything unfolding. You can watch them come and go. Allow yourself to observe this natural ebb and flow, rather than diving into the depths to engage with the melodrama in your mind.

As you cultivate a sense of curiosity, you'll notice the patterns of your thoughts, the sensations in your body, and the emotions that arise, but now you'll be able to refrain from participating in them. When you sense your mind wandering, gently guide it back to the simple act of noticing where you are. Over time, this practice brings a sense of calm and clarity that allows you to move through life with grace and ease.

Remember, meditation is not about stopping thoughts, but about being the observer. Behind it all, you'll find a profound sense of stillness amidst the chaos of your thoughts.

YOU ARE THE SKY

you are the sky—
vast, blue, infinite, neutral,
clear, open, and constant.
everything else is the weather—
thoughts and emotions moving like clouds.

sometimes your mind is clear
other times, clouds consume you,
but they are not you.

you are not your thoughts.
you are not your emotions.
you are the one who experiences them.

the clouds will come and go—
with calm or with chaos,
yet you remain as the vastness that holds it all.

you are the subject,
and your thoughts are just another object you are aware of.
you are the one who witnesses the world unfolding,
who watches the storms roll in
knowing they soon roll out.

so when life feels chaotic,
when the noise rises
and the storms crowd in,
remember: it's not your job to prevent the weather.
be still and let the clouds pass.
steady and unchanging,
the sky remains.

—you are the sky

SELF
(inner conflict)

intuition	>	**conditioning**
a deep, internal knowing		back-and-forth thinking
sensing in the body		operating through the mind
subtle, persistent nudge		loud guilt-trip
transcends reasoning or words		justifies and second-guesses
speaks through peace		tones of fear
guides you toward what is good		believes its protecting you
from God		from past experiences/expectations
knows		argues
body feels open and light		body feels constricted and tight
stepping into the unknown with faith		clinging to the familiar out of fear
true self		conditioned self

—*trust your intuition over your trauma*

[E] NERGY IN [MOTION]

An emotion lasts for only 90 seconds, if we let it.

Emotions are just energy in motion. They arise and then dissipate
like waves. Understanding this changes everything. When we look
at an emotion as passing energy, rather than an overwhelming state
of being, then suddenly sadness, frustration, anger, grief, and fear
become less paralyzing.

The problem is that most of us don't let emotions pass through us in
90 seconds. Instead, we hold on.

We overthink, analyze, and question, turning energy into a story.
Those stories shape our thoughts, which settle into moods, and
then solidify as identities. "I *am* sad," we say, when sadness was only
passing through. When we don't let emotions move, they get stuck in
our bodies. We become blocked.

The source? Overthinking.

As someone who loves to understand everything, thinking seems
safer than feeling. Thinking keeps us in our heads, where we try to
fix emotions and create distance from them, rather than allowing
ourselves to experience them fully in our body.

But what if you let yourself feel discomfort for 90 seconds and then
let it move? We can do anything for 90 seconds. When emotions flow
freely, they stay fluid. But when we hold onto them, they become
beliefs we carry that filter how we perceive the world.

The practice is simple: instead of running from your emotions with analyzing, I invite you to open your heart. When you shift from your head to your heart, ah—now you're closer to the core of it all. You see where the reactive energies come from. You don't need to know why it's here or how long it'll stay. Simply let go of judgment, stay present, and allow the energy to move. Place your hand where you feel the emotion in your body for extra support and breathe through it. When you do this, something incredible happens. The tightness lets go of its grip. The fear softens. Your mind and body relax and open up, and you can see the moment before you with compassion instead of fear. Suddenly, the emotion passes.

So next time discomfort arises, don't try to think your way out of it. Get out of your head and sink into your heart. Slow down and breathe through it. No labels, no words, no fixing. Let the energy flow in. And let it flow out.

Because that's all it ever wanted to do.

CREATE SPACE

may you soften the edges of fear or anxiety by gently allowing it to take up

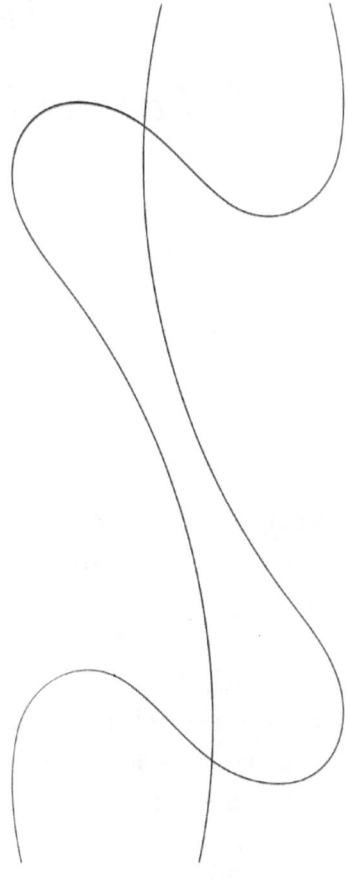

space.

IV.

WATER with BALANCE

One evening, as the sun dips toward the horizon and warm light stretches across the garden, you notice it—a small break in the earth. A sprout.

At first, it is barely there, a delicate sliver of green emerging from the soil. But it is proof that beneath the surface, in the quiet darkness, life was taking root. Your watering was working. The seed had to break open before it could grow, surrendering its old form to become something new.

A sprout is fragile, its stem thin, its roots still finding their way. It needs water, but not too much. Sunlight, but not too harsh. You step back, remembering that *balance* sustains life. Just as the garden thrives through the rhythm of rain and sun, of blooming and wilting, growth requires both effort and rest, movement and stillness, surrender and care.

You, too, are learning the rhythm of balance. Some days, that means reaching outward, embracing movement, expression, and action. On other days, it means drawing inward, resting, and trusting that even in stillness, transformation is taking place.

You take a deep breath and watch the wind move through the trees. You realize: you are not separate from the garden. You, too, are a part of creation, ever-changing, ever-growing. This is how life unfolds. Not without challenges, but in harmony with them. Healing is not about eliminating struggle; it's about learning to hold everything with openness—the waiting, the growing, the breaking open, the becoming.

And so, you keep watering. You keep showing up. Because the sprout will not rush, nor will it resist. It grows in balance, held between what nourishes it below and what calls it above.

| AND |

all or nothing thinking
often holds us back,
keeping us stuck in a limited mindset.

the truth is
many things often co-exist.
many things can be true—at once.

you can be sad *and* healing.
you can feel an emotion *and* not act toward it.
you can move with both effort *and* ease.
you can love someone *and* do what's best for yourself.

you can care about someone *and* still feel hurt by them.
you can be angry *and* grateful.
you can be gentle *and* strong.

you can not like where you're at *and* still trust that things are working
out as they need to.
you can be grieving *and* still find joy.
you can miss something *and* know it wasn't for you.
you can do your best *and* still hurt someone.
you can be getting better *and* still need improvement.
you can be content *and* still want more.
you can mess up *and* still be succeeding.

nothing is black || and || white
like we often perceive.
many truths co-exist.
one perspective has many different facets and angles.

let it all be there.
let it all exist.
we liberate ourselves when we realize
we can be all of it.

THE MOUNTAINS WERE MY FIRST LOVE

I've found the mountains to carry a deeply masculine energy—a presence that is strong, rooted, and ruggedly unchanging. There is a quiet power in their steadfastness, the way they hold their ground no matter the storms or seasons. Looking up, you feel this solid presence. A reminder of endurance, of time stretching slowly through changing seasons and growing trees. The mountains are silent witnesses to centuries, unmoved by all that shifts around them. They know what it is to be still, to be certain.

The ocean, in contrast, hums with femininity—mysterious, alive, always shifting. She teaches me fluidity, a kind of expansive strength that is soft, yet fierce. The sea is never the same; she ebbs and flows, rises and falls, showing how change is a rhythm, a dance. Her beauty lies in her movement, her openness, and her flow. She invites surrender, proving that strength is not always about standing firm but somehow about yielding, adapting, and becoming. She is a wild force that cannot be contained, always vast, powerful, and untamed.

The mountains remind me of the importance of my roots, of knowing who I am even when the winds of life try to sway me. But the sea, she teaches me to flow with grace, to let go of what I cannot control and find strength in softness. Her rhythm is not one to be conquered; it is to be experienced and surrendered to.

One was my first love, an unshakable grounding force that taught me how to endure, even when the world seemed to shift beneath me. But then the ocean found me tired and weary. With her ever-changing currents, she rocked me, saying there is power in softness, too. She taught me that life is a rhythm to be felt rather than resisted.

In this balance of forces of masculine and feminine, we find our true potential. Like the yin and yang, they are not two opposing forces but complementary.

Roots and flexibility, strength and softness, endurance and surrender—we need it all. Together, they allow us to blossom fully. To stand tall like a flower, yet remain soft enough to dance with the wind.

Life's beauty lies in being both rooted and free.

LESSONS FROM THE TIDE

I've spent 365 days sitting at the foot of the ocean—
studying, observing, learning, feeling, releasing.

my conclusion?
the sea is very much alive.
a living, breathing entity
[God's lungs.]
an exhale
breaking and crashing on the shore,
followed by an inhale
retreating, returning to the sea.

the ocean is calming, yes,
but, more often, expressive.
have you ever seen the ocean
angry?
it's one of the most unapologetic things to witness.
waves thrashing themselves against the cliffs,
loudly roaring and raging without shame.
untamed and powerful.

studying the ocean has taught me how to ride the wave of emotion.
to let the energy rise and swell as long as it needs to
without fear or apology
until it crashes.
to let it move
instead of holding everything in or down.

giving us permission and space
for whatever we need to feel:

calm and chaos,
stillness and storm.
the sea holds space for it all—
       something we, as humans, often struggle to do.

why are people drawn to the ocean?
perhaps because we don't know how to be that vulnerable,
       how to be that raw.

the ocean shows us what it means to feel deeply
and to keep moving,
to embrace our depths
without apology.

PENDULUM

The pendulum swinging is a necessary part of healing that is rarely talked about. It's the process of recalibration—swinging between extremes as you work toward a place of balance.

If you've spent years neglecting your own needs, overextending yourself, and saying "yes" to everything, the initial shift might feel drastic. You may find yourself pulling far in the opposite direction, becoming highly protective of your time and energy, and reluctant to give to others, feeling like you have nothing left to give. Give yourself grace; this phase won't last forever. This is just what it looks like to unlearn burnout and relearn balance.

Slowly, you'll start giving again. And no longer in a way that makes you feel depleted or from obligation, but rather from true joy and desire.

If you used to numb or suppress pain, healing can unlock a floodgate. It can feel like you're constantly crying or suddenly angry all the time. But this wave is part of the release. Eventually, you learn how to sit with emotions without being consumed by them.

At first, things might feel like they're swinging between one extreme to the other—but this is part of the process of finding a healthier middle ground.

Healing isn't linear; the pendulum will continue to swing back and forth as you learn, adjust, and grow. Over time, the swings will become gentler, and the extremes will soften. Trust the process.

Eventually, the pendulum will find its natural resting place, a harmonious middle ground where you feel balanced and aligned with your authentic self. This middle space isn't about perfection but about finding a rhythm that honors both your needs and your desire to connect with and support others.

Be patient with yourself as the pendulum swings. Each swing will guide you closer to that balanced and grounded center.

LIFE LESSONS FROM YOGA
(to take off the mat)

1. Move between effort and ease.
2. Balance strength with softness.
3. Rest is productive. It allows you to seal the benefits of all your movement.
4. Breathe through hard postures.
5. Don't think about what's next. That will bring you into the future and just add stress. Focus on your next breath and be present to the pose you're in.
6. When you're trying to balance, find a focus point to keep your gaze on. *(God)*
7. Notice what's happening within you without language or words. No judgment, just take in the raw sensory data.
8. Push yourself to your edge and be willing to try new things.
9. Be flexible.
10. Every day is different. Honor where you are today.
11. Ground down to rise up. Stability comes from rooting yourself firmly before reaching higher.
12. Practice over perfection.
13. Don't compare your progress to others. Listen to your body and what you need.
14. Set intentions, not expectations.
15. Make sure you're in alignment.
16. Open your heart.
17. When you fall out, get back up.
18. Enjoy being present in your body.

BE OPEN TO IT ALL

In yoga, I notice my heart, throat, and hips reflect a posture I long to
embody—
open, wide, expansive, spacious.
This openness is a disposition I long to carry with me.

I desire to be open to all of life,
not just the parts I prefer.

It's easy to resist something and label it as "bad" when it doesn't align
with my limited idea of what should or shouldn't happen.
It often feels like a battle, as though I'm waging a war within myself
constantly trying to decide what to let in and what to keep out,
opening my heart to the good and closing it to the bad.

This endless judging is exhausting. Always deciding, guarding,
controlling.
What if, instead, I let it all flow through me?

To trust it's all unfolding, moment by moment, as it's meant to.

So today, dear life,
I open myself to you—all of you.
I welcome with open arms what I once labeled *bad* as much as what I
deem *good*.

I embrace the peace alongside the chaos,
the joy as deeply as the rage,
the love as tenderly as the grief.
Every experience is here to teach, heal, and liberate us
and God uses it all.

PART IV:

REACHING UPWARD

awakening to God as light
and source of all growth

"As the sun shines both on the cedar and the smallest flower,
so the Divine sun illuminates each soul."

—St. Thérèse of Lisieux

Early morning spills across the garden, golden and full of promise.

You step into its warmth, feeling the hush of something sacred in the air. The sprout, once a fragile sliver breaking through the soil, now stands taller, its leaves turning ever so slightly, in the direction of the sun. It does not force itself upward. It does not resist. It simply reaches. Not by fear or by striving, but by design. Something written deep within. An instinct, a calling, a quiet knowing. It has always been meant for this.

And so have you.

Like this fragile stem, you are drawn toward something greater, something unseen yet deeply known. There is a light calling you forward, inviting you to rise.

For so long, the seed was hidden beneath the surface, surrounded by darkness. In those early days, when nothing seemed to be happening and waiting felt endless, the light seemed absent. Like God was distant. But now, breaking through the surface, the sprout knows what was true all along:

The sun was never missing.

The seed just couldn't see it.

But now, you feel it. A pull to open, to rise, to trust. The flower does not push itself upward; it simply follows the light.

Reaching is an act of trust. It requires extending beyond the safety of the soil. It is not always easy. The sprout must withstand the wind, the changing seasons, the weight of its own unfolding. And yet, it does not resist. It leans in.

This is the moment of realization. You are no longer closed off, but open. No longer stuck, but free. No longer in the dark, but standing fully in the light. And in that light, you are held. You are guided. You are deeply loved.

So you, too, reach toward the Light that is the source of all growth.

SOURCE

A tree's growth is not dependent on the unpredictability of the weather, but on the source from which its roots draw life. Its ability to produce fruit comes from something beyond itself.

In the same way, when you place your confidence in God, you're like a tree planted by the water. With roots that reach deep underground, you draw nourishment from a never-ending supply.

It's easy to get exhausted as seasons of life shift unpredictably. But the tree that is planted near the stream does not wither in drought because its life is not sustained by external fleeting circumstances. It is sustained internally. By something deeper, something constant, something that never wanes.

This is the life of faith. Trusting in God is not about escaping hardships, but about being anchored in something greater than the storms. Your gaze must always be fixed upward.

Unlike a tree planted in shallow soil, which relies solely on rain and risks being uprooted by the winds, when you abide in God, you are firmly established. Your strength comes from the Living Water, flowing beneath the surface, nourishing you even when everything around you seems barren. You naturally move from a place of scarcity to abundance when you are connected to a source that never runs dry.

Through the heat, your leaves remain green.

In droughts, you continue to bear fruit.

This is the paradox of faith. The world may expect that hardship will make a person wither, yet those who remain close to God flourish even in adversity. The strength to endure does not come from within ourselves, but from being connected to the One who is the source of life itself. Your roots reach out, not in desperation, but in gentle trust, knowing that even when you can't see the water, it is there.

Growth in the spiritual life is not about striving—it is about *abiding*.

A tree does not strain to grow; it simply remains planted where its roots can access the water daily. In the same way, when we remain rooted in God and draw our sustenance from Him, we will find ourselves growing, stretching toward the light, bearing fruit in every season.

THE LANGUAGE OF GOD

Walking barefoot along the shore,
"listen," intuition said.

All I heard were waves crashing and people laughing. A seagull caught
a fish, and a little girl ran into her father's arms.

Some might say God doesn't speak to us.

But I heard everything.

FAITH IS NOT A FEELING

I have felt so weak, so fragile, walking through those heavy church doors.

I've barely had the desire to stand or to pray out loud. And to sing? Absolutely not.

Tears silently rolled down my cheek as I listened to the Gospel. A sadness overcame me for wanting to resonate with the hope and promises being spoken. But in the moment, feeling far from it.

And yet—there is something profoundly beautiful about the Church as a whole. Each member making up the body. Although I may not know the person sitting next to me or behind me, I hear their prayers, I hear their worship, I hear their trust. And on days when I can't muster the words, I can remain still. I can just show up. And I can let them carry me.

Showing up, especially when you don't feel like it, is a way of declaring an intense truth with your actions:

My faith is stronger than my feelings.

My faith is more anchored and steady than my feelings, so I can depend on it to be more true. I'll pray the prayers and I'll show up, even when I'm struggling to believe in the promises of the Lord. Even when the words I'm speaking or hearing don't feel true. Even when my hope is hanging on by a thread and I'm angry at God. Even when doubt feels bigger than the belief that things can and will get better.

Feelings are ever-shifting and always moving through us. So perhaps on the days when I feel confident about God, maybe that same person who was full of hope last week and carrying me is now holding onto the hope in my voice, my proclamation of faith.

Oh, how we carry each other.

I write this to the person whose feelings seem bigger than their faith. It's okay. It is human, even good, to have doubts, to have seasons where hope feels slim, and to still know that your faith is separate from all of that. It can stand amongst it all. Your faith can handle the waves of passing negative thoughts and emotions. In these seasons, we learn that God is not a feeling. Our faith is not a feeling. We often base our decisions—what we do or avoid doing—on emotions that are ever-changing and fleeting.

To the person who has ever walked into a church and felt unwelcome to come as you are, with these very normal and human struggles, *I see you.*

To the person who hasn't felt the energy to show up, *I get it.*

To the person who feels too resentful to worship, *I understand.*

You are welcome, always, and I'm sorry if anyone has ever made you feel anything otherwise. Because especially on those days when you don't feel it, the Mass is medicine for the soul. The Eucharist, God dwelling within us in the most physical way, overflows our being with grace, healing, and strength, beyond what we can understand or be able to tangibly feel or conceptualize as we receive it.

So much happens in the spiritual realm that we can not see or feel, but your testament of just showing up is an act of faith, an act of courage to hope in the "more" you do not feel in the moment.

Because feelings are only fleeting.
The discouragement, despair, doubt, anxiety—all of it is fleeting
but God is not.

—this will pass, yet God always remains

MATTHEW 7:4

I'll never understand how some of the most religious people I know can also be some of the most judgmental. It's so paradoxical. One human is not of any more value than another. It's not our place, as other *flawed* humans, to stand on a pedestal pretending to be the Divine. Each of us is carrying our own burdens, imperfections, and struggles.

What *is* our place? To practice the same mercy constantly poured out on us and to always throw our arms open wide. We are all living the journey of the prodigal son. We get lost in our wanderings, too. And if we were given other people's situations, we might make the same decisions we currently condemn.

It's the judgment and hypocrisy pouring from God's people that often pushes others away from wanting to have a relationship with God at all. I've seen it too often, and it never stops breaking my heart. So many have been hurt, distanced from their faith, or have turned away from God because of those who misrepresent Him with pride, piety, and shame, and then claim it's in His name.

But we see Jesus live in a radically different way. He eats with the sick and the sinners, befriends the outcasts, the addicts, the prostitutes— the ones who have been cast aside by society and, too often, by people of the Church. He doesn't look for perfection, rather He seeks the broken, the hurting, the ones who need healing, and there He is most present.

Before pointing a finger, we have to remove the plank from our own eye. Each of us carries our own addictions and defects, too, and we must be careful because pride is often the most dangerous of them all. When the need to be right overshadows love, it can block God's voice. In those moments, we become so consumed with ourselves and our beliefs that we miss the human heart beating and hurting right in front of us. This is where spiritual damage happens.

Humble yourselves, dear Christians. We are all in need of the same mercy. It's only when we stop pretending to be the Judge, and become the loving hands and feet of Jesus, that we reveal God's heart to the world.

And to those of you who have been hurt and pushed away by judgment or hypocrisy, I am so sorry. Please hear this truth—God is Love. God can't be anything but Love. Humans, even good-intentioned ones, are flawed. But God is not.

God is waiting with open arms, always ready to embrace you in His boundless love. God is not an "I told you so," but rather a "Welcome home!" His love doesn't come with conditions, and His voice does not echo in judgment or disappointment. God never speaks in shame, confusion, or condemnation. He doesn't speak in anxious tones or tremble with fear. Instead, His words are full of peace and He aches for you to come back to Him and experience the reality of who He is—nothing but Unconditional Love.

YOU SAY

I say, "this disqualifies me from love."
You say, "Not Mine."

I say, "this can't be forgiven."
You say, "It Already Is."

I say, "I can't be loved,"
You say, "Child, I Can't Help But Love You."

I say, "you can't love me in spite of my brokenness,"
You say, "I Love You Because Of It."

SPOKEN INTO BEING

God does not speak in suggestions.

Every word spoken by the mouth of God—
becomes.
creates.
is.

"My peace I give you" is not advice. It's not God crossing His fingers, hoping you eventually find some comfort and relief. In that very moment, peace is given to you. It takes hold. It becomes yours. Fear doesn't stand a chance.

Divine words do not return empty. They accomplish what they are set out to do.

When God said, *"Let there be light,"* there was no pause. No hesitation. Instantly, light was. Darkness shattered at the command.

Like the stars and the sky, when you were spoken into existence, no mistake was made. Every detail—your crooked smile, the way you feel things so deeply—it's all intentional by the Artist. You are not an accident, nor are your emotions something to suppress. The depth of your heart is not a flaw but a reflection of the One who created you.

Just as rain falls from the sky to nourish the earth, bringing seeds to grow and flowers to bloom, so too does every word from God bring life. It never falls flat or returns void. What God speaks takes root, fulfilling the purpose it was meant for.

So if God has spoken love over you—a whisper of truth, a nudge toward something greater, a call to step forward, an anchoring phrase for your doubts—know that those words are not just fleeting thoughts or a hopeful sentiment.

They are real. They are already unfolding.

God does not plant desires in your heart without providing a way to fulfill them. If a truth has stirred something deep inside you and God has placed a longing in your heart— for peace, for healing, for something new— then He plans to bring it to fruition with your *yes*.

Maybe it was a moment of clarity, a word that resonated in your soul, or a longing that won't go away. Pay attention. That voice, that feeling, that pull toward something greater is there because it was spoken over you and is happening to and for you.

Your life has purpose.
Your longing is not in vain.
What He has begun in you, He will bring to fruition.

These promises of hope, peace, mercy, healing, and new life are your birthright, your Divine inheritance. They are not distant possibilities or mere hopes for the future. Even now, they are unfolding, taking root, and coming to life within you. What God has spoken over you is already in motion, preparing to bloom in His perfect timing.

Your being alone, darling, is an intentional word, breathed into existence with love.

DIVINE INTIMACY

Please don't settle for a faith with no heartbeat.

If you approach God from a place of obligation or duty, rather than as a deeply transformational and intimate relationship, you're missing the point completely. We reduce our relationship with God to a checklist. Similar to tasks at work, we check off an allotted time of prayer or church on Sundays like an obligation completed, a project turned in. But nothing deeper is there.

Imagine coming home to your partner and crossing it off a list after you spend an hour with them. Nothing kills a relationship quite like that.

The problem is we leave no room for God to breathe or move. God cannot surprise us, speak into our day, or stir something within us because we've placed a box around when and how He's allowed to work. We ask for answers, but don't wait to listen, and then call Him absent. We confuse Him as a God of the past, not a God of the Now.

I beg you—*don't take the spontaneity and intimacy out of your relationship with God.*

What we fail to understand is that the Divine is very much alive. Like any relationship, connection with God needs spontaneity, intimacy, vulnerability, and moments of unexpected grace. It involves real emotions like feeling frustrated or not heard, hurt, or disappointed. It requires honest expressions like "I love you," "I'm sorry I hurt you," and "thank you for all you do."

Scheduled time for communion with God is a beautiful thing, but what makes a heart fall deeper in love is often the way we catch our Beloved gazing at us when we aren't even looking. It's finding love notes left in unexpected places. It's the spontaneity and the surprise. It's being pulled in by their presence, and missing them the second you aren't with them. It's the desire. It's wanting to stop everything you're doing to be present to the person in front of you.

It's the all-encompassing want of connection. It's only wanting that person after a long day. It's noticing the small details you admire. Our relationship with God is not a monologue or one-sided. It's the dance between two. Speaking and listening, giving and receiving, pursuing and being pursued.

My point being, without room for spontaneity and intimacy with God, you'll only experience a half-assed version of what's possible in the relationship. Intimacy is more necessary than "doing" all of the right things.

This pursuit is not bound by time or space, so it doesn't matter where you are. God is not only present in a church, and prayer is not only when you are on your knees. The deepest prayer comes through unfiltered tears, doubts, or questions, and rarely starts with a sign of the cross. It can never be crossed off or "finished." It's eternal.

Your relationship with God is as alive and moving as the wind around you. We don't know His next move, but the beauty is in the mystery. God's pursuit of us is relentless and wild and surprising in every way. Don't lose sight of the romance of it all because you're too busy "maintaining" your faith.

Let God romance you every once in a while.

How the Divine makes itself accessible to us?

I'll never get over it.
It never stops stealing my breath and captivating my heart.

—*the greatest love story if you open yourself to it*

LIVING WATER

two things in the world
can *soften* me
without fail:

the ocean
& the eucharist.

—*both living water*

SOUL REST

In its purest form, prayer is essentially rest.

A deep, soul-soothing rest. The kind you ache for.

It's the place where you can stop striving and worrying, and just be present to Who is already present to you—Unconditional Love—who deeply sees and knows you more fully than anyone else.

Prayer is a relationship with God. Just as no two relationships are the same because each person is different, prayer is a personal and unique experience. There is no "right." Prayer is not a technique, it's a disposition of the heart. You don't need to follow a script or perfect a formula. A string of pretty and put-together words, no matter how beautifully spoken, becomes empty if your heart isn't in it.

When distractions come, and they will, don't judge yourself. Gently return to awareness that you are in God's presence. Let your heart rest in the assurance that it's not your effort or ability to focus that makes prayer effective, but rather God's love for you. You don't need to be a certain level of holy or get everything "just right" to connect with God. It happens naturally and effortlessly. You may not feel or hear anything special, but that doesn't mean you aren't spending time with God.

It's not about controlling your mind, but rather gently opening your heart.

You can take a break from trying to figure everything out, and trust in the One who holds all things together for your good. You can release everything you've been gripping so tightly to and trust that the

Divine is working, even in the unseen and the unknown. You can stop pretending to be God, and let God be God. Feel the exhale in that.

To lay back into the arms of your Creator is to enter a place of dependent trust. Just as a child naturally leans into the embrace of a parent, secure in their love, protection, and provision, you can rest in the unwavering love of your Heavenly Father.

This exchange of love is not about invoking God to come closer, but realizing He is already here, ever-present with and in you. His presence is constant, unwavering, and never dependent on how aware you are of it or how good you've been. His nearness is not something you can earn or create. It's a reality that exists right now.

It's like stepping outside and noticing the sun on your face. The sun was there long before you looked up, but when you become aware of it, you feel its warmth, its light. God's love surrounds you, whether or not you are conscious of it. God's love for you still exists, even in the times when you don't believe in it. When you take a moment to pause and recognize it, your heart can open to receive the love and peace that has been there all along, waiting for your invitation to draw near.

Unlike our relationships with other imperfect human beings, God doesn't withdraw. He doesn't leave. He doesn't withhold. God's love isn't selfish or insecure. It is never concerned with "Self." It's never disengaged. The more you cultivate this awareness, the more you live in the reality of God's constant nearness. You may drift, but He remains.

Prayer is not about asking for something, it's about spending time with Someone.
It's not about making a list of requests, it's a relationship.

It's resting in Unconditional Love. Love is always at work in you,
quietly transforming and healing, even when you don't notice it.

Remember, prayer is not about what you do—
but rather what *God does in you.*

To remain in God's love,
that's all prayer is
after all.

SELF-RELIANCE

God can do far more
with
your surrender,

than you can do
with
your control.

THE FREEDOM OF DETACHMENT

At 21 years old, not even a college graduate, I found myself standing in my best friend's room just days after she unexpectedly passed away.

Her soul was no longer here on this earth. Yet, as I looked around, everything was exactly as she left it. Laundry hamper half-full. Clothes still on the floor; yoga pants inside-out from rushing out the door for, what she didn't know would be, the last time. Receipts for shoes she needed to return in her purse. An unfinished to-do list sat on her desk with only half of the boxes checked off in freshly dried ink.

That moment changed me forever.

I learned, so early in life, that we don't take anything with us when we leave. My perspective shifted irreversibly, and from that day forward, I felt a profound sense of detachment from the world.

At 21, you think you're invincible. You're in the prime of youth, surrounded by dreams and possibilities. To go through such a life-shattering experience at that age was a surreal realization of human fragility and our impermanence. Our possessions, our clothes, our money, our accomplishments, what we have done or still need to do—none of it comes with us. None of it really matters.

The things that feel so urgent and important now will not even be a thought during the moment that awaits us all. Anything can happen at any time, even to the people you'd never expect. And I've found that not to be scary, but a reality that has changed me, making me want to be intensely present in every moment.

During a time in my life when the world seemed to expect me to jump headfirst into climbing the corporate ladder, none of it seemed important. I watched my peers post celebratory updates about landing their first jobs, while I was just trying to find my way out of bed in the morning.

I came to realize that all that truly matters is *relationships*—our relationship with God, with ourselves, and with others. The impact we make on one another is really the only tangible thing we leave behind. That's it. Nothing else.

When people ask about my 5-year, 10-year, 20-year plan, I admit "I have no idea," as awkward silence fills the air. It's not that I don't have goals, dreams, and desires. I absolutely do. But I know that even if I had a step-by-step plan of how to get the house with a white picket fence and 2.5 kids, life would not necessarily follow my playbook, nor should it. I'm not in control, so I've stopped pretending to be. I lost the one person I never thought anything would happen to.

Courteney had so many beautiful plans and dreams: grad school, marriage, having children. But her trip on this side of Heaven got cut short. Way too short, in my opinion. Maybe on time, in God's (that's something I'll never stop wrestling with). See, Courteney dreamed of the future, but never at the expense of cherishing every second of the present.

I have found that God radically wrecks our plans. There are sharp turns I followed that I would have never imagined for myself. Because of those seasons of life that I couldn't have even planned if I wanted to, I am a completely different person, in a way I'm so grateful for. I am being shaped every day by what God has for me. I no longer waste energy on limiting life based on my near-sighted vision and trying to micromanage it all to align with what I want, just to feel more secure. I have desires and dreams, but now I hold them loosely. I'm okay with not knowing the route to get there, or if I ever will, because I'm just grateful for the opportunity to be on the journey at all.

I constantly have to practice letting go of the need for control. I have to remind myself over and over again to trust in the unseen GPS guiding my path. I'm not the driver, and that's okay. Every second of life's wild and beautiful road trip is meant to be savored, not meticulously planned, feared, or worried about. So for now, I slip off my shoes, put my feet up on the dashboard, roll down the windows, and feel the sun on my face.

Enjoy the ride. Relish every stop along the way, even the ones you don't expect. You'll get to your destination soon enough.

—*Court, I can't wait to squeeze you when I get there*

IN HIS HANDS

God takes care of
everything.

—a reminder

I DON'T KNOW MUCH

I don't know much in this life,

but I know God's voice.

And on most days,

that feels like enough.

BEYOND THE SELF

Spirituality is not just another pursuit to take on or a hobby to explore.

It's not another thing to get *into*.

The whole purpose of spirituality is not to accumulate more, but to let go, to surrender, to be set free.

It is a journey of getting *out*—
out of your own way,
out of your will,
out of your ego,
out of your pride,
out of your need for control.

It is the path of freeing yourself from yourself.

True spirituality is about losing yourself—
    not in emptiness, but in Truth and Fullness.
    not in confusion, but in Divine Mystery.
    not in nothingness, but in something Infinitely Greater than you.

It is about stepping beyond yourself and into God.

OPEN HANDS

This is your reminder to move with openness and grace.

Every time you try to control life, peace slips through your fingers. To live from a place of flow is far more freeing than living from a place of grasping. Peace naturally follows when we release the grip on how we think things should be, and open ourselves to the beauty of how things actually are.

Life isn't meant to be lived in the confines of our mental narratives, where we stress about making everything outside align with what we think we need to be okay inside. Wouldn't you rather participate in a wild, beautiful, and unpredictable life? One full of unexpected blessings, challenges that help you grow, and moments of grace, rather than to live inside your head of expectations and miss the whole thing?

When we allow ourselves to submit to the unfolding of each moment as it is, we can freely receive the ways we are abundantly provided for as we walk along. It's a lot better than clenching our fists tightly, attempting to make life succumb to us.

I will never stop singing the praises of the power of surrender. It's been the most transformative and spiritual practice in my life—a quiet yet powerful invitation to trust the unknown. When I reflect on the moments and decisions that have brought me the deepest joy and growth, they are almost always experiences that were guided by something much greater than myself. The experiences that shaped me the most and had the greatest impact weren't anything I would have ever chosen for myself initially. They were a call from God that I tried to decline again and again out of fear, until it became undeniable that it was a leap worth taking.

The truth is, the most beautiful chapters of my life unfolded in ways I couldn't have predicted or imagined. They came when I let go, stepped aside, and allowed life to lead. What I thought I wanted or needed paled in comparison to what was waiting for me. Instead of constantly striving for what we think will make us happy or secure, surrender allows us to receive what is truly meant for us—often in ways that are far richer and more fulfilling than we could ever dream.

Keep your hands and heart open to what God has for you. You'll be completely amazed at what is placed in them.

SUR·REN·DER (v.)

surrender:

to open to
what's here.

to let go of
the resistance.

a loosening
or opening.

to let go of
the clench.

an inner capacity
to release the grip.

to make room
for the flow of life.

a willingness to say yes
to life's unfolding.

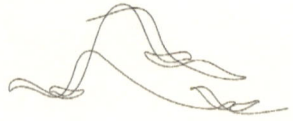

THE PRESENCE OF GOD

You can't be by the ocean
and still believe God is
not good.

IN OCEANS DEEP

I first learned to recognize the voice of God as the one calling me out into deep waters, drawing me to venture outside of my comfort zone.

Each time I've felt that familiar tug on my heart, it's as if the Divine was standing on the shore, beckoning me to leave the safety of the sand and step out into the expansive seas ahead. His call usually involved doing the harder thing—the choice that required me to depend on something far greater than myself, beyond my trust into the great unknown.

"Follow the sign of a white flower for your college decision, even if it leads you to the Midwest."

"Go on a mission trip to the Andes Mountains in Peru."

"Experience homelessness in Washington D.C. instead of going to the beach with your friends for spring break."

"Be a missionary after college. You'll talk to people about God, fundraise your salary, and move wherever they place you instead of taking that corporate job."

"Take the opportunity to understand addiction more closely."

"Face your vulnerability. Put your heart and grief on display, and write the book."

"Pack your car and move to the West Coast without knowing a soul."

It's exhilarating and terrifying, all at once.

His voice has urged me to dive into situations where I had no experience, to speak up when my voice trembled, and to embrace change when I longed for stability. It's in these moments that I've learned the beauty of reliance—not just on my strength, but on His. Each leap into the unknown is not just about overcoming my fears, but trusting in a greater plan, even when I can't see what that is.

Just like Peter on the boat, I've felt that time and time again, God has asked me to leave the safety of where I am and walk out onto the water. Keeping my gaze fixed on Him, rather than on the unsettling waves, is what has kept me from sinking.

There's really no way to make sense of it to others when you get that pull in your heart. The people who loved Peter and couldn't hear Jesus calling him would, of course, have lovingly cried out, "Stay in the boat!" out of concern for his safety. He looked radical and crazy for stepping into the water. But Peter knew if God was calling him to venture out, then He would provide for him.

Although it had been a dream forever, when I finally moved to California in my late twenties, I still wondered why I was led there. What hard thing would I be asked to do next? I braced myself for a challenge, anticipating the next bold move, the next ocean to dive into.

But as I settled into this new space, something unexpected happened. It turns out, the Lord's voice is much softer in this season.

It's not the urgent, thunderous call I've known in the past, the one that propels me forward with purpose and momentum. No, this time,

His voice is quieter, more gentle, like a soft breeze whispering through the palms and waves washing calmly upon the shore.

"Rest, without feeling guilty."

"Learn to receive joy."

"Let yourself be loved."

"Be still."

"Return to being childlike, and collect seashells."

"Laugh again."

While the call here doesn't feel as intense as those before, it feels just as important.

In this season, God is asking me to slow down, to heal in the simple moments, to let myself feel joy, and to trust that His plans for me are unfolding in the stillness. It's a different kind of adventure. One where the challenge is to quiet my soul enough to hear His voice, even when it doesn't come with fireworks.

But to remain, to sit in the stillness, requires something deeper. Sitting with the parts of yourself that you may want to run from is hard. It means choosing to believe that there is beauty in the slow work of transformation and in the gradual healing that happens when we allow ourselves to be seen. It's here that true healing begins, not in the hurried busyness of avoidance, but in the willingness to be still and let His light reach the darkest parts of our hearts.

Sometimes, His greatest callings aren't about the external battles we fight, but the internal peace we cultivate. And perhaps that's the hardest work of all—to let go of the need to always be moving forward and instead, allow ourselves to be held by grace. Right where we are.

I'm forever learning that just when I think I have begun to grasp the depths of God's nature and understand who He is or what He will do next, I am always surprised. His mystery is endless, and His ways are far beyond my understanding.

May I always remain open to His Divine surprises, never confining God's voice and calls to the limits of my expectations. May I always allow God to be so much bigger than I'll ever be able to know.

PROMISES OF HOPE

the tulips breaking through the soil
planted last month
promise, *"better things are coming."*

the fresh morning sunlight
after a long winter
whispers, *"it will be okay,"*
as it dances in through the blinds
to wake you up.

the first sip of warm coffee
comforts, *"it will get better,"*
on an untouched day.

"it will work itself out,"
declares a new month ahead
with a fresh calendar
and a blank journal page.

"maybe you don't feel it right now,"
suggests the sun sparkling on the waves
shimmering to the album of the tide,
       "but it will all be okay, my dear."

THE LORD PROVIDES

If God transcends time and space, then isn't He already in your future?

See, God isn't in the dark like we are. The future isn't uncertain to Him. Nothing takes Him by surprise. There is a deep comfort in knowing you are never arriving anywhere alone. Rather, you're stepping into what He's prepared for you. God will never lead you somewhere only to abandon you.

God knows your unique fears and your restless thoughts. He knows your every desire and need. Not just the universal longings, but the deeply personal ones. The ones you hesitate to put into words. The worries that keep you up at night.

He already knows how everything unfolds like where you'll live, the job you'll take, and the people you'll meet.

And most importantly? That you'll be okay.

God knows the things you've dreamed of since you were a kid. He knows the deep longing in your heart to be loved by someone who loves Him above all else, even more than they love you. He knows the past moments that have shaped your future hesitations, and the disappointments that have made you guard your heart.

He isn't indifferent to the way uncertainty unsettles you, or how the unknown makes your chest tighten and your thoughts spiral. He knows that even when you long for something new, stepping into it can feel paralyzing—that you wrestle between wanting to trust and fearing what's ahead.

God knows you hate change and that you crave stability and security. And because He knows, He prepares. He lays stepping stones before you, softens the landing, and sends moments of peace—before you even realize you need them. Because He knows you fear change, He will cushion your transitions, just as He always has—with people who feel like home or a peace that surpasses understanding.

These are the details we assume God overlooks, the complexities we think He couldn't possibly understand. But He does. And in His love, He is already preparing what you need, exactly how you need it.

In every season of life, I can look back and see the specific people God placed in my life at just the right time. I believe He hand-selects who and what we need in every situation. I have seen the ways He made what seemed impossible to get through, looking ahead, suddenly manageable when I took it day by day.

The things that will make you feel safe, and comfortable, and joyful— those are the details He's working out right now.

When we worry about the future, the lie we're often believing is, "What if this is as good as it's going to get?"

As I asked this in prayer, a gentle, all-knowing voice overcame me. "This is just the beginning."
You'll just continue adding to all of the beautiful things in your life.

So next time you're paralyzed by fear, remember, God is already in your future. If He calls you somewhere, He will provide for you there. Even before you arrive. He is faithful in every season.

God is already there in the places you're afraid to go,
in the comfort you can't yet feel,

in the plans you haven't yet made,
in the conversations you've yet to have.

If there's one thing I continue to learn in every unique season, it's
this—

the lord provides.
the lord provides.
the lord provides.

PART V:

GROWING TOGETHER

*cultivating a garden
of connection and relationship*

*"A flower cannot bloom without sunshine, and
a man cannot live without love."*

—Max Muller

Hands resting gently at your sides, you're watching the flower you've nurtured from the very beginning as it has grown tall and strong, petals open wide and in full bloom toward the sun.

You reflect back to when this place was different. This garden used to be overgrown with weeds. Thick, tangled, suffocating the life beneath. The soil was barren, hard, unyielding. For a while, it was easier to believe the weeds would never be uprooted or that this ground would always stay barren.

But deep inside, you knew something greater was waiting for you.

You slowly pulled the weeds, one by one. You softened the earth. You planted a seed of self-love, even when you weren't sure if it would ever take root. You continued to show up every day to water it with patience and presence, with mindfulness and balance. And then slowly, quietly, life began to emerge and the flower rose to meet the sun.

At first, it was just one sprout, fragile and small. You tended to it carefully, being inspired by the way it stretched toward the light, its petals slowly unfurling with time.

For so long, it felt like you were tending to this flower alone. Like this was your single patch of earth to care for, your own quiet work.

But as you rise to your feet here and now, the wind shifts, and something changes.

A petal brushes against your arm. Then another.

You look up.

The garden is full.

All around, flowers have bloomed—tall, wild, radiant in every color and every kind. How have you not noticed until now? You were never alone in this. Others have been here all along, planting, tending, nurturing their own seed. They have been growing beside you, even when you were too focused and didn't see them.

For so long, you nurtured the soil, watered the unseen roots, tended to what was growing even when you couldn't yet see it. You learned to trust the process, to let go of what no longer served you, to make space for new growth. And now, you see the fruit of that labor. Not just in yourself, but in everything around you.

Colors spill across the landscape in wild, effortless beauty. Some flowers are just beginning to open, their petals unfurling with quiet courage. Others stand tall, fully bloomed, their presence steady and sure. Each has taken its own time and had the courage to start over, again and again. Each one is belonging and breathtaking.

This is how it was meant to be from the beginning.

For so long, you have been growing—breaking through, learning to trust, opening to the light. And now, you see the fullness of what has been unfolding all along.

This is Eden.

Not a lost place, but a promise restored. A return to what was always intended. The flowers do not compete. They do not strive. They grow side by side, flourishing in the presence of one another. You feel it in the air, in the warmth on your skin, in the way the flowers lean into one another without fear, without hesitation.

No flower blooms alone. No soul was ever meant to grow in isolation. The beauty of the garden is not in one single flower, but in all of them together. Each one looks different, but all are planted in the same earth and growing under the same Sun.

The whole garden is in full bloom—not just one flower, but many, standing together in the light.

A TREE SOMEWHERE

in
some
quiet forest,
a sequoia tree
took root on the exact
day you were born.
beneath the soil, its roots began
intertwining with others,
forming a foundation of strength.
just as the sequoia reached impossible heights
by leaning on those around it
so
have
you.

—you were never alone

FRIENDS

As I dance through my twenties, while sparkly heels in dirty bars are traded for bare feet curled up on the couch, I am so deeply in love with my friends. Ones from all seasons of life. People gloss over friendships focusing on romantic love. They throw themselves into work and identify themselves by their careers and accomplishments.

How sad to be skimming over some of the most underrated and important chapters.

The bricks that have built the foundations of my twenties have nothing to do with men or jobs. It is the friendships that have carried me through. It's the people who water my flowers that don't have to, and yet, still choose to.

When I look back, I'll hold close the women who have healed what they did not break. Your twenties are for living with your best friend and running errands together. It's eating leftover pizza in the kitchen at 2 am after coming home from a night out. It's having multiple closets to choose from and fighting over which playlist you'll do your makeup to.

As we grow up, tag looks like road trips across the country to see the lives we're independently building, as we cheer each other on from opposite coasts—from every hardship to every celebration.

It's the strangers you meet in new cities that you get to reinvent yourself with. It's friendsgivings, and dinner parties, and "who can make the best cocktails" with the once-strangers who are now family.

I've moved to a new state without knowing a single soul multiple times now,
and if there's anything I've learned; it's this:

Love is **abundant**.

People will love you and you will love them,
wherever you go.

—*friends are the family you choose*

ROOM TO BLOOM

cherish the relationships
where you are both
constantly
in a state of
b e c o m i n g.

those who resist
change and growth
in you or themselves

   f

      a

        l

          l

             away with each metamorphosis and cocoon   shed.

people who hold onto the idea of
what you inhabit
in a given season
and grasp too tightly
onto who you are
for their security
and the role you play for them,
that there is no space
for transformation
instead of allowing room
for *g r o w t h,*
will not make it into
your upcoming chapters.

you'll come across people who
grip too tightly to their complacency
and scold you for threatening what it shakes within them
when you grow and change.

but isn't it the greatest joy
to sit across from a person you love
noticing how they have shifted?
how they are
better,
kinder,
more confident,
more honest,
and more at peace
than once before?

how they are more
themselves.

why would you not want
to be surrounded by people
who also want that for you?

because you cannot truly
!celebrate! another
if you're stuck within yourself.

make the space to witness different versions of each other
and walk through varying seasons together,
celebrating what falls away and what comes along.
let's celebrate each other through all of the seasons.
let's grow (together).

humans are constantly becoming
and unbecoming.
love every version you get to witness
of the people in your life
and hold tight to those who do the same for you.

SEASONAL

Isn't there a melancholic kind of gratitude toward the people who are no longer in your life? A breaking that caused pain in a moment has now created room for more aligned people to enter in and love you in the way you need. You slipped through the hands of those who had no clue how to hold you, allowing you to grow separately in the ways you both needed. This doesn't diminish the joy and gratitude for the years when they were exactly the right person to cross paths with. You look back with no resentment, just an understanding of fondness and love for those people in that season and what they meant to you.

I used to take things personally. I would chase, ask why, overexplain, and apologize for what wasn't mine, trying to make sense of someone's distance. I was the one to always keep reaching out. But with time, something shifted within me. When I stopped reaching out, I saw what naturally fell away. It showed me the relationships that were one-sided. Letting go and not chasing anyone as the door ricocheted has been one of the biggest gifts to myself because I look around at who is at my table now and I couldn't be any fuller. Every person I now get to break bread and toast wine glasses over loud laughter with is each person I didn't know I needed.

I'm so lucky.

Thank you for the space you made.
I genuinely hope your table is filled with people that make you just as full.

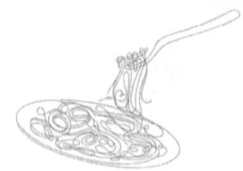

CLIMBING THE LADDER OF LIFE

I think there's a reason we don't go through the same things at the same time.

Life is a ladder.

Sometimes, you find yourself a step or two higher, with the stability and strength to reach back and extend a hand to someone who's feeling the weight of the climb. Other times, you'll find yourself a rung lower, exhausted, and on a slippery stretch needing that steady hand to help you up. We're all just climbing together, taking turns needing a hand.

This constant exchange, this ebb and flow of support, keeps us connected as we all move forward. No one stays on top or at the bottom for long. We're each rising, falling, and lifting one another along the way. What a relief that there's always someone to reach back when we stumble to steady us, or to help lift us to the next step when we can't muster the strength alone.

You may be in the best season of your life, while your best friend or mother is in the worst season of hers. The worst year of your life may be the year of endless blessings and dreams-come-true for someone else. But this imbalance is natural; life has a way of keeping us each on unique paths, so we're able to support one another.

The beauty and fluidity of it all is that nothing stays the same. Seasons change. The hard times give way to relief, the easy times yield challenges, and the good and the bad ebb and flow for everyone. No one is spared from sorrow, and no one is denied moments of joy. Our lives move through rhythms, carrying us through peaks and valleys.

Together, each step becomes lighter, because we're all going to the same place.

—we're all just walking each other home

MY PEOPLE ARE NOT MINE

When you pick a flower, it dies.

Once vibrant and reaching toward the sun, its beauty begins to wither in your hands. What was meant to grow freely, to dance with the wind and drink in the rain, is suddenly cut off from the very things that sustain it.

Similarly, the people in my life are not mine.

They are not here to complete me,
nor to revolve around my world.
They exist with a purpose far beyond my own.

If I love someone truly,
my desire should be not to keep them to myself,
but to help them step fully into the life they were meant to live—
a life that is not mine to claim.

What a beautiful gift it becomes, then,
when they cross my path unexpectedly
and land in my ever-so-lucky, open hands,
free to be given or taken away at any time.
Never mine to clutch,
only mine to cherish.

In prayer, I often find myself pleading
asking God to stay close to the people I love.
I beg Him to heal their wounds,
to calm their hearts,
to fill their days with peace, joy, and abundance.

But in my longing, I sometimes forget
God already desires these things for them
far more than I ever could.

The Creator doesn't need a reminder
to take care of His creation
and love the very ones He breathed life into.

My mom is God's Beloved,
before she is my mom.

My dad is God's son,
before he is my dad.

My friends, my brothers, my partner, my future family,
the people that I so fiercely love and want to protect—

they are Yours, God,
way before they are ever mine.

—you can take better care of them than I can

MOM

your defiant irish will
runs through my veins.

your unfiltered sense of humor
runs in my blood.

the way your father taught you
to wear your heart on your sleeve
has led to my also seemingly sensitive skin.

your constant song
has birthed me with a love for singing
and an impulse to dance in the rain.

you taught me devotion
and you showed me adventure.
you taught me class
and you showed me grace.

you instilled in me
your love for the sea.
you infused me
with dreams and aspirations
to go for it,
the spreading of my wings.

your independence
to color outside the lines of rules,
to experience life more fully
(and sneak into hotel spas),

has given origin
to my own
wild h e a r t.

no one can take
away
the ways in which
we are
deeply connected
by blood & love.

time
and space
defy these things
so inherent and rooted.

our loyalty does not expire
with the breath in our lungs.
our love does not dissipate
with our time on this earth.

i was knit in your womb
with strands of your stubbornness
and DNA of your resiliency.
you knew me before
i came
and i will know you long after
you leave
because i carry you with me
in my flesh and bones.
a lineage of strong women
that put breath into my lungs
and a beat in my heart.

thank you,
mom.
you are a part of me
always.
and i,
you.

LIFE WRAPPED

What if, at the end of our lives, we were shown a list of statistics measuring how we lived?

As you took your last breaths, the charts would blink, showing:

The people you brought closer to God, inviting them to feel deeply loved and known. The souls you unknowingly inspired, leaving encouragement in places you never imagined. How often you were fully present in the moment with those in front of you.

The emotions that colored your days most frequently—whether joy, peace, grief, or gratitude. How often you chose kindness over being right, even when it was hard. How many times you forgave, especially when it was difficult. The number of times you swallowed your pride out of love.

The times you overcame fear to choose courage, no matter how scared you were. The number of dreams you pursued, even when the odds were against you. How many meals you shared with loved ones, a table full of wine, cheers, and laughter. How often you listened to God. The times you were called kind behind your back.

When you stood up for what was just, even when it was unpopular. When you did the right thing, even when no one saw. How many seeds of hope you planted, even if you never witnessed them grow. The moments you chose love, in its many forms, over fear.

Maybe, if we knew the true measurements of a successful life, we'd slow down. We'd pay less attention to things measured by the world's standards and honor how we live and love in the quiet, sacred, and often unseen moments of life.

Perhaps, in the end, the statistics that matter aren't about how we lived, but how we loved.

CREATIVITY

it's ironic when people say they aren't creative because they can't paint
or draw—

humans create every day as their way of existing.

we make meals, and memories, and children. we design homes and
flower bouquets in our kitchens. we curate playlists and outfits. we
draw conclusions and paint pictures with our words. we make love
and we build cities.

a woman is the most creative creature on earth.
knitting another sacred being in her body—without even a thought as
to how.

so you may not be able to play the guitar or write,
but god darling,
you create life with your very bones.

—don't tell me you aren't creative

BREAKUPS

"so what do i do, now?" she asked.

    every morning,
    you swim in the sea,
    letting the crisp water
    wake you up
    and remind you
    that you're alive.
    you drink in the sunshine
    and wild salty air,
    you inhale with the tide
    and exhale with the crashing waves.
    you walk slowly,
    collecting seashells
    of your favorite colors.

my darling,
    you keep.

    that's what you do
    in the uncertainty.
        you *keep.*

    you keep going.
    you keep waking up.
    you keep trusting,
        even if you can't see.
    you keep breathing,
        even if you're shaking.
    you keep walking,
        even if you don't know where you're being led.

you meet new people,
and squeeze the ones who have always been there
when you need reminding of who you are again.
you write in your favorite coffee shops
and buy flowers for your kitchen.
you paint your walls yellow,
you explore the city,
and you learn from the incredibly gentle pace of nature.

you make a deal with life
to trade your fear for excitement.
and you find yourself
again.

that's what you do.

and in return,
love will find you
again.

        i

   r   *s*

because soon enough, the fog will   *e*

& the sun will reveal it all—
you've had everything you needed within you all along.

—*break-ups*

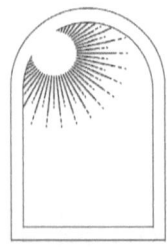

EMPOWERING LOVE

you once confused love as the oath:
"you take care of me,
and i'll take care of you."

but what if the promise is
"you take care of yourself.
i'll take care of myself.
        and when we need help
        we ask each other."

love does not mean...
        make me happy.
        regulate my emotions.
        do the things i don't want to take responsibility for.
        feel the hard things for me.
        adapt into every role in my life.
        fix my problems.

love transcends the transactional.
true intimacy comes from mutual respect and responsibility.
it waters autonomy and personal growth.
love is fostering a partnership
where both individuals are willing to do the work,
face the challenges, feel the pain, and grow independently.

love says, i will your good, even when it's hard.
i am with you as you do the hard things for yourself.
i am here for you,
supporting you,
always,
and i am also empowering you
to support yourself.

A PATIENT LOVE

you won't find someone
who never triggers you
or doesn't upset you at times.

rather it's about how someone holds space for you
in those moments.

are they patient
and soft?

do they never grow weary
of kissing your
wounded places
over and over,
finding new and beautiful
constellations of color
in the bruises each time?

it's not about finding a perfect person
who meets your every need
and whose stuff doesn't hit your stuff,
because that's impossible.
but look for someone who can
gently hold whatever comes up,
holding a flame to your walls of self-defense
melting them into nothing but sweet, warm
honey-dripping love.

someone being patient with you
on your bad days
is the softest form of love.

LET ME CARRY IT

if i could take your pain
and carry it myself,
i would.

i'd strap it to my back,
carry it up the mountain,
feeling it in my bones
as if it were my own—
if it meant you could breathe
without the weight pressing down,
even for just a moment.

if i could step inside your heart,
i'd throw open the blinds
and sweep away the cobwebs.
on the days you're too weak to make it into the sun,
i'd come over and water your garden
tending to the soil,
and nourishing the cracks and roots
when your strength feels too fragile.
i'd carry the weight of the watering can,
pouring in love and patience
for each place to grow.

it isn't fair
that the world demands this of you,
that you must endure what feels
unendurable.
i want to rewrite the rules of the world
where suffering can be divided

and loads can be shared.
i'd shoulder it all,
just to see you at ease.

i would rather carry your pain
than sit in my powerlessness.
nothing hurts worse than
seeing you hurting.
i can sit by you and hold your hand
but to not be able to take it
from you feels cruel.
seeing you in pain
feels more unbearable than
carrying the pain myself.

it's a love that aches
because it longs to be able
to do more.

if i could,
i would take it all.

DON'T SETTLE

Please don't settle for a drop of counterfeit love when you have access within you to the Well that quenches your deepest thirst. Don't settle for mediocre or half-assed. Don't entertain anyone who makes you feel less than, with your messy, lovely details.

Stop feeling like you're asking for too much when communication and consistency are the bare bones. You deserve a fiercely loyal love and a steady hand. Stop settling for the bare minimum and calling it good "enough." You are worthy of more than fleeting moments or half-hearted gestures. You deserve Sunday coffee and flowers, slow dancing in the kitchen, and god forbid, you deserve answered texts. You deserve someone to make a lot of love & a lot of life with.

It's out there waiting for you and it's also within you, all at the same time. This love will embrace you with its warmth, ensuring you never feel like an afterthought or an option. It's the kind of love that honors your time and feelings, and never stops pursuing you.

So move along from the half-hearted form of mediocre attention, and trust that this love exists in abundance. May your hands and your heart be open to recognizing it when it arrives—because it will show up and let you know just how lovely you are.

If anyone dims your light or asks you to shrink, if you find yourself defending your worth or you're left wondering, don't just close the door. Slam it. Don't just walk away. Run.

When you stay connected to the source of Love, a drip has no real value.

LET THEM

Each person is on their own unique journey, and it's not our place to decide or control their path.

We don't always know what's best for others, and it's necessary to allow them to be exactly who they are. Love them for who they are, not who you wish them to be. Just as you are on your own journey, so are they. Let others feel their emotions, have their reactions, and make their own decisions. Their experiences and choices are theirs to navigate, not yours to control or fix.

At the same time, don't let anyone hold you back from expressing yourself, pursuing your goals, or honoring your calling. Stay true to who you are, and allow others to do the same.

Let someone...   Let someone...

- be angry   - disagree
- have a reaction   - not want to
- feel their emotions   - say no
- be upset   - make their own decisions
- throw a fit   - not respond
- walk away   - have different beliefs
- cope how they need to   - take time to process

Real love is about allowing someone to be exactly who they are—without conditions, without expectations, without the quiet pressure to become a version that fits your mold.

When you release the need to manage others, you set them free.

But more importantly, you set yourself free.

GET THE TATTOO

My twenty-first birthday was one of the best weekends of my life.

I was the only one in my high school friend group to go to college out of state. On that special day, surrounded by my college friends, I suddenly saw my tall, beautiful best friend walk through the door, her smile lighting up the room. I couldn't believe my eyes. She had pulled off traveling thousands of miles to surprise me, even though we talked daily. I hugged her so tight, not believing my eyes. Then, she asked me to help her with a cake outside, and there, standing next to it, were two more of my friends. Three of my closest friends from home had flown out to surprise me. They planned the whole thing, and I had no idea.

That weekend, my world collided with the people I loved most. We spent hours talking about getting tattoos—a way to carry each other with us, no matter where we go. But as the weekend slipped by, we never found the time to make it happen.

You hear people talk about tattoos all the time, telling you that you'll regret it as you age, or that your taste will change, and you'll wish you hadn't. After all, it's permanent.

Later that year, my best friend tragically passed away in a car accident. The same girl who had confidently walked through those doors, just four months before, was gone. At her funeral, I longed for something to tie us together in a physical, earthly way—something permanent.

My regret? Not getting the tattoo.

It's ironic, really. It shows how we often regret the things we're too scared to do, rather than the things we did but wish we hadn't.

So, my advice? Go on that trip. Say yes to the adventure. Do that thing with the people you love while you can.

Get the tattoo.
Don't worry—it's only as permanent as life.

HAPPY BIRTHDAY

you left at the age of 21 years old.
as i write this, you'd be 28.

but isn't life at 28 so different than life at 21?
and isn't life at 56 going to be so different than life at 21?

i once heard that every seven years
the cells in your entire body are destroyed
and replaced with new cells.

that means that who you would be today
would be a different person
on a cellular level.

would we even recognize you?
would you recognize us?
life changes so much in your twenties
& we're all just trying to figure it out
as we try to gracefully transition from one season to the next.

your birthdays are still filled with so many questions,
so many *what if's.*
i can't help but be consumed with the wondering.

>   who would you be?
>   what would your life look like?
>   would you be married? what job would you have?
>   where would you be living? would we be roommates?
>   would you have a baby? or three?
>   would your hair finally be as long as you wanted it to be?

how would you have grown even more confidently into yourself?
how would our friendship have grown?
how would we have navigated our twenties alongside each other?
what advice would you have given me over the past seven years?
most importantly, what would we be doing tonight to celebrate?

your laugh would be more distinct than our memories,
you wouldn't be what feels like almost an idea,
or a beautiful, untouchable dream.
a stranger i am unceasingly searching to find in every crowd
that has the slightest resemblance of you,
realizing you are the most alive in my subconscious now.

every year i'm caught off guard by how painful these days still are
as if there are set dates in the calendar year when you trip
and the scab opens and starts bleeding again.
i guess some things will never make more sense, no matter how much
time passes.
maybe the pages of our grief diaries never truly come to an end,
because the love never ends?
the relationship never ends?

you, sweet friend, never end.
happy birthday, court—
for as long as we exist, so do you.
i'm not sure the rules up there, but i hope you can see how many
people are celebrating you today and every day.

—we're growing up, but you're still 21

RESERVED

to the person who has been called "shy":

> perhaps you are not shy at all, but rather you are just picky about who you choose to spend your time with.

> perhaps you are "reserved" because you want to reserve—(v.) preserve, retain, withhold, save— energy for people who can meet you on the same level of depth that you live from.

> perhaps you don't want to waste your energy or time sharing yourself with people who are not available to receive or understand you.

> it's okay to be picky with your circle.

> it's okay to not reveal all of yourself to everyone.

> it's okay to prefer deeper connection over more acquaintances.

> it's okay to prefer fiercer love, with fewer people.

> it's okay to reserve yourself for the right people.

reserve away.
reserve deeply.

UNPACKING TOGETHER

"thanks for telling me
you were anxious.

you could have dealt with it on your own,
but it's better we unpack it together."

—*words that healed years of feeling too heavy*

ACKNOWLEDGE THE PAIN

I think people rarely want advice.

Most of the time, we just want our pain to be seen.
People just ache to hear, "I'm sorry, that's hard,"
rather than a list of solutions.

Until we've lived through the same experience as someone else,
we may lack authority to speak into it with any real understanding.

If you are married,
don't tell your friend
that their singleness is a gift
or there will be blessings from their divorce.
          Simply acknowledge the ache.

If you are not in someone's family dynamic,
don't tell them how to navigate it.
          Simply acknowledge their struggles.

If you don't personally struggle with what someone is facing,
resist the urge to prescribe answers.
Acknowledge that you don't know what it's like for them—
and you are still there to listen.

If you are on the outside looking in,
you have no degree or expertise
to make any kind of judgment.

I can tell that the people who judge others for how they cope often
lack the depth that comes with lived experience. They haven't lived

through profound loss, betrayal, or despair. The only lens they can see through is their own.

The tendency to judge others' coping mechanisms often comes from a place of misunderstanding, one rooted in privilege or distance from real pain.

It's often those who have never truly *had* to cope themselves.
People who have never been plunged into the depths of pain,
the kind that forces you to do whatever it takes to survive.

It's easy to criticize
when you're watching from the sidelines,
cozy in your comfort,
and not on the battlefield.
It's easy to say, *"Well, if it were me, I would—"*
when it's just a thought in your head
instead of a reality at your feet.

Your judgment carries no weight,
no validity,
no depth,
until you've walked in those shoes,
on that exact path,
with those exact burdens pressing into your shoulders.

To judge from the safety of comfort is easy.
To understand from the depths of experience
is something else entirely.

(Thank you
for your opinion
though.)

LONELINESS

loneliness is not a defect
specific to you alone.
it has existed since God took adam's rib
to create woman, declaring
it is not good for man to be alone.
loneliness does not point
to a sign of brokenness,
but rather a condition of humanness.
it's simply a longing
of good desires within us;
pointing beyond the self
to something
greater—

our loneliness says,
"i want my life to be in service
to something bigger
than myself.
there is more than this,
there is more
than me."

it's a gentle reminder
that your heart beats,
and you've always yearned to give
the boundless love you carry.
your flowers overflow with water,
eager to spill life
into another garden.

we all experience loneliness
from time to time.
& maybe in that we can recognize
we are not so broken,
we are not so
different.
we are not so
a l o n e
after all.

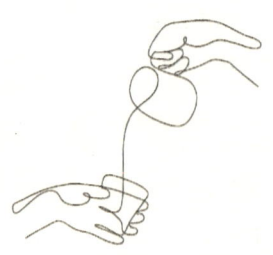

I HOPE YOU'RE OKAY

When I say *"I hope you're okay,"*
I guess what I mean is—
I know you're not okay.
But I hope the sadness
does not completely envelop you today.

I know you're left wondering
how you will ever pick up all these pieces
and feel whole again.
But what I mean is,
I hope you have a few quiet moments
where the light breaks through
and an exhale feels easy.

I hope you are being soft
and gentle with yourself.

I hope you find the compassion
and patience to treat yourself
like you would a child.
I hope you find the courage
to wash the day off,
wrap a blanket around your tensed shoulders,
let a cup of tea warm your hands,
get some sleep,
and try again tomorrow.

I know you don't feel okay
but I hope you see something
that makes you smile

for the first time in a while,
and you think of something that
makes you laugh out loud.
I hope the weight of what you're carrying
is one pound lighter today.
And that I can lessen it
however possible.

I know that
you're not okay,
        but I hope you know
        you're not alone.

HUMAN DIGNITY

to see the other requires us
to momentarily take the gaze
off ourselves.

in looking down at each other,
we create pedestals,
declaring a greater and less than.

it is only from humbling ourselves
in the act of looking up,
that we can
a d m i r e.

to truly love
is not to have attachment to positions,
roles in relationships, or status.

to serve
not out of piety
or privilege.
but an honest
reverence
and adoration
for the other.

humble yourself—
love *requires* it.

our parents care for us in our youth,
and in their later years,
we stand beside them in the same way.

although in posture you may be looking down
at the sick in a hospital bed,
at the poor on a street corner,
at your loved one in pain,
may you continue to look *up*
from your soul to theirs.

always
find
something
to
admire.
no matter how small
and hold onto that.

for this—
is how to maintain
the *dignity*
of the human person.

LOVE DISGUISED

you're searching for love,
but darling,
it has shaken your hand a dozen times today.

your best friend sent a song that made her think of you.
a handsome stranger held the door with a smile.
your roommate brought home a coffee, with extra cinnamon, how
you like it.
your mom texted, "thinking of you," this morning.
the old man at the grocery store showed you a picture of his sweet
wife.
your yoga teacher complimented your progress.
your dog showered you with kisses when you got home from work.

you're looking everywhere for love,
but what if it's never left your side?

—*love surrounds you*

ANSWERED PRAYERS

how beautiful it is to know
in this very moment
you're living out
one of the most beautiful chapters of your life?

you don't have to wait
until you can look back
to notice.

—you're living answered prayers

IN FULL BLOOM

look at you—in full bloom.

no longer waiting for the sun to rise,
no longer wondering if the rain will stay,
you have learned to trust both.

you stand tall, petals wide,
soft yet strong,
bending with the breeze, but never breaking.
you have mastered the art of being both rooted and free.

you live in a garden
where love grows wild,
where laughter spills like sunlight,
where your roots run deep in the soil of belonging.

you are surrounded—
by hands that have held you,
by voices that have lifted you,
by hearts that beat in rhythm with your own.

this life is no longer a distant hope,
no longer a wish whispered to the wind.
it is here, it is real—
a place you have built,
a home you have nurtured,
a dream you wake up living.

still, the petals open wider.
still, the fragrance carries on the breeze,

reaching beyond what you can see.
you are in full bloom.
and yet—
there is always more to come.

You've arrived.

You look out to all you have created from taking the time to slow deep, sink deep within, and trust yourself. The scent of all types of flowers drift on the breeze, and for the first time, you realize—this garden wasn't just about the flowers.

It was about having the courage to begin again.

It was about the tending. The trusting. The becoming.

Every season has shaped you. Every moment of showing up, even when you couldn't see the change, mattered. It wasn't about reaching the destination, but about who you became along the way. Empowered. More loving toward yourself. Softer. More open to the light.

A quiet knowing settles in your chest. The growing is never over. The seasons will change, the winds will shift, and new seeds will take root. And when they do, you will be here. Clearing. Tending. Nurturing. Trusting in the unseen.

Knowing, now, you can do it.

You rise, brushing the earth from your hands, and turn toward the path ahead. The garden stretches far beyond what you can see, bathed in golden light.

And so, you keep walking—growing, blooming, becoming.

Always.

—This is just the beginning

Sending You on Your Way

As you turn the final pages of *Words that Water Flowers*, my hope
is that you've found moments of peace, clarity, and inspiration to
carry with you. Writing this book has been a journey of its own, one
filled with prayer, reflection, and a deep belief that God works in the
quietest and most profound ways.

It's my prayer that you are leaving this space with a renewed sense of
self—a knowing of the beauty and potential that resides within you.
We all grow in different seasons, and I pray that as you continue on
your own path, you do so with the awareness that every step, whether
slow or swift, is part of the sacred unfolding of your life.

Thank you for allowing my words to accompany you. May you find
strength in surrender, beauty in your brokenness, and grace in your
growth. And always remember: You are enough, just as you are.

As you close this book and continue your journey, remember that
growth is never a straight line. It's a winding path, full of moments of
blooming and moments of quiet stillness, both necessary.

Know that every seed you've planted—whether it's in your heart,
your relationships, or your work—is being nurtured by the hands of
a loving Creator who sees you through every season. Be patient with
yourself, for you are always growing, always becoming, always being
held.

May you walk forward in the confidence of who you are, rooted in the
love and grace that is already within you. Keep choosing to grow with

courage, letting your roots sink deep and your flowers bloom in their time. The world is waiting for the beauty only you can offer.

With love,

Katherine

AUTHOR BIO

Katherine Plucinsky is a best-selling author based in San Diego, California. In her books, *High Tides & Open Hands* and *Words that Water Flowers*, her writing explores the power of surrender and finding strength in vulnerability. Deeply committed to faith and personal growth, Plucinsky's work encourages readers to trust the unfolding of becoming—whether in stillness, breaking, rooting, or rising. She believes that healing is not about achieving perfection, but loving better. Through introspective poetry and reflective prose, she offers words that nourish the soul. Katherine hopes to inspire a deeper and more honest connection to God.